THE
GOD WHO
IS REAL

THE GOD WHO IS REAL

A CREATIONIST
APPROACH TO EVANGELISM
AND MISSIONS

HENRY M. MORRIS

FOREWORD BY DON RICHARDSON

BAKER BOOK HOUSE
Grand Rapids, Michigan 49516

Copyright 1988 by
Baker Book House Company

ISBN: 0-8010-6233-0

Third printing, April 1989

Printed in the United States of America

Contents

Foreword

Dr. Henry Morris and his associates at the Institute for Creation Research in San Diego, California, have for many years been evangelical Christianity's foremost defenders of creationism. Many professors in the natural sciences who had grown arrogant in their espousal of evolution as *the* answer to the question of origins have been shocked to find formerly complacent students raising strong objections to the theory of evolution (more properly macro-evolution) based upon their study of ICR materials. Even as early as the 1970s, articles were appearing in *Scientific American* and other journals acknowledging that ICR-sponsored initiatives were forcing secular educators to realize that they and their humanistic ideas could no longer ride roughshod and unchallenged over the minds of modern youth.

With this latest work, *The God Who Is Real*, Dr. Morris first summarizes the arguments for special creation and a personal God from the natural sciences and then widens his investigations into arguments derived from the social sciences. Finally, he shows from the Scriptures and from history that the God of creation is the living Christ of the Bible.

I do not merely recommend this book; I urge it upon readers who want to keep abreast of an ongoing struggle that should concern us all. I especially recommend it for open-minded and intelligent people who are searching for the true God and true peace of soul.

Don Richardson
Author of *Eternity in Their Hearts*

Introduction

The purpose of this book is to help people understand why they should consider and then believe the saving gospel of Jesus Christ. The Christian faith cannot be just one religion among many, for it claims to be the only true revelation of the Creator of the universe. It is either the only true religion or else completely false, so no one can remain neutral concerning it. An abundance of objective evidence in support of its claims has been offered by Christian scholars over the years. Serious-minded people, therefore, owe it to themselves to at least look at the evidence. If true, it could make an eternal difference in their lives.

Because of its unique claims, Christianity has always been a missionary faith. The final command of Christ to his disciples was to go "into all the world, and preach the gospel to every creature" (Mark 16:15). Thus, Christianity is not really Christianity if its adherents are not diligently trying to win non-Christians to faith in Christ. Consequently, from the first century on, Christians have scattered around the world preaching Christ.

This missionary thrust has been more successful in some countries than others, but converts have been gleaned in almost every tribe and nation. Various missionary approaches have been tried, and different schools

of thought have developed—even whole theological systems—regarding evangelism and missions. Most of these
are not succeeding well today, however, and the world is
drifting further and further away from the true God as
revealed in the Judeo-Christian Scriptures.

If the premise of Christianity is right—that is, if the
Bible really is the infallible Word of God and Jesus Christ
really is the only true way to God as he claimed (John
14:6)—then the Bible should also show us the best way of
reaching people with this truth. I have attempted in this
book, therefore, to follow the example of the apostles
themselves, as set forth in the Bible, in carrying out the
evangelistic purpose mentioned above.

When we look at the example of the first Christian
evangelists and missionaries, as reported in the Book of
Acts in the New Testament, we find that they *have*
shown us the best way. When Paul and the other apostles
preached the gospel to the Jews, they invariably preached
from the Old Testament Scriptures. In the synagogue at
Thessalonica, for example, "Paul, as his manner was,
went in unto them, and three sabbath days reasoned with
them out of the scriptures, opening and alleging, that
Christ must needs have suffered, and risen again from the
dead; and that this Jesus, whom I preach unto you, is
Christ" (Acts 17:2–3).

Paul could reason with them from the Scriptures because they, like he, already knew the Scriptures and accepted them as the Word of God. With this common
ground, he could use the evidence of fulfilled prophecy—
especially as centered in Christ's resurrection from the
dead—and many of his listeners believed as a result. This
approach was commonly used by the apostles when they
witnessed to Jews who knew and believed the Bible.

When they addressed Gentile pagan idolaters, however,
their approach was altogether different. Such people neither knew nor believed the Scriptures, so it would have
been futile to use them as a basis for their case. Instead,

the apostles began on the common ground they shared with these polytheistic pantheists: the evidence of the Creator in his creation.

For example, at Lystra in Asia Minor they urged the people to turn back to the true God with these words: "...ye should turn from these vanities unto the living God, which made heaven, and earth, and the sea, and all things that are therein: who in times past suffered all nations to walk in their own ways. Nevertheless he left not himself without witness, in that he did good, and gave us rain from heaven, and fruitful seasons, filling our hearts with food and gladness" (Acts 14:15–17).

Similarly, in Athens, surrounded by the evolutionary philosophers of the Stoics and Epicureans, Paul preached to them about their "unknown God," saying: "God that made the world and all things therein, seeing that he is Lord of heaven and earth, dwelleth not in temples made with hands" (Acts 17:24). He then emphasized God's creative sovereignty over all nations, climaxing his message with the great assurance of the unique authority of Christ, evidenced by the fact that God "hath raised Him from the dead" (Acts 17:31).

The first method, reasoning out of the Scriptures, is appropriate for many church audiences in the United States and other Christian communities, since these people for the most part still believe the Bible and know something about its teachings, even though they may not yet have accepted Christ as personal Savior.

The second method, however, is more appropriate for people brought up to believe in one or another of the world's great non-Christian religions. Even in the so-called Christian nations the younger generations have been so indoctrinated with evolutionism and humanism that most of them reject the Bible and know little or nothing about its teachings. Following the biblical premise, such people need first to be approached on the basis of creationism, showing them the fallacies of their evolutionary atheistic or pantheistic premises and the strong case for special creation of all things by the omnipotent God whom they still sense in their hearts to be real. Then they can be introduced to Jesus Christ through the testimony of the resurrection and, finally, to the Holy Scriptures as the inspired Word of the Creator, revealing the saving gospel of Christ to a lost world.

Many missionaries have testified that evolutionism is the chief hindrance to the effective preaching of the Christian gospel everywhere. Since most of the world's religions have always been fundamentally evolutionary systems, rejecting or ignoring the concept of an omnipotent, personal Creator, their adherents have easily adjusted to modern evolutionary "science" and have now become more resistant than ever to the preaching of the cross of Christ. This is especially true among the young people and educated leaders of the various nations and tribes. Many Christian nationals have said that a primary need in their own countries is a real creationist revival.

I have written this book with this situation in mind, hoping it will meet this very real need. Thus, the first part of the book deals largely with science, documented with the words of evolutionists and humanists, and establishing the strong case for creation. The latter part deals mostly with spiritual matters, documented by the Word of God as it explains the great truths of God's grace and salvation.

It is my prayer that this small book with a grand theme will help lead many readers to eternal life as they place their trust in our Creator and Savior, the Lord Jesus Christ.

1

The Impotent God of Chance

When a person first begins to search for true meaning and purpose in life, he encounters the awesome task of sorting through all the religions and philosophies of the ages to try to decide which to believe. At first this seems impossible, and the easy way out is either to go along with what one's parents believe or give up the search altogether. Many opt for one of these, with little thought of any consequences.

However, for those who really want to know the truth, the task is not too difficult. There are, after all, only two basic religions: either there is one true God who created all things or there is no real God at all.

The Choice of Gods

Here are the two alternatives. The universe was either created or it was not—one or the other. If it was really created, then the one who created it called into existence the entire universe of space, time, matter, animals, people, and any other supposed gods that may exist. There can be no other real god if this God actually created everything. He is the Creator—the God of all the cosmos.

If the universe was not created, but has been changing or evolving or oscillating endlessly over the ages, then the

13

universe itself is the ultimate reality. In effect, it takes the place of God. There is no real creator at all, although new forms of being may be evolving out of older forms within the eternal cosmos. Some modern philosophers have even proposed that the cosmos may originally have "created" itself, by a "quantum change in a primeval state of nothingness," in which unlikely situation the assumed primordial nothingness becomes the equivalent of God.

In any case, the choice becomes one of believing either in a Creator—an omnipotent, transcendent, personal God who created the cosmos itself, with its magnificent array of complex systems and living beings—or in the eternal cosmos evolving itself into this array of complexity. The first of these two basic choices does not state who the Creator is, what methods he used, or when the creation took place. The second choice does not state how the cosmos evolved itself, what its present character means, or what future destiny awaits it.

Since there are only these two basic choices, however, it should not be too difficult to look at the arguments for each and then make a decision. It is like coming to a fork in the road and deciding whether to travel east or west. Other decisions may arise later, but for now you only need decide whether to start down one road or the other. You cannot travel both roads at once.

The Two Religions

The choice between God and "no-god" means a choice between two world views—two religions, if you will, or two philosophies of life. The first is centered in the Creator as the maker, ruler and judge of all things, to whom we, his creatures, are responsible for our thoughts, words, and deeds. If we hold this God-centered world view, every decision and action should be oriented toward him and his purposes in creation.

The second world view, based on faith in the cosmos itself as the ultimate reality, is centered in nature and, ultimately, in man as the highest attainment of nature's processes. Thus, man himself becomes the measure of all meaning in life. This man-centered religion may involve worship of nature as the "creator" of man, worship of the state (corporate man), or even veneration of some great leader or teacher as representative man.

We can identify these two competing religions as theism and atheism. Since the former implies one—and only one—omnipotent God who created all things, it is really equivalent to monotheism (one God). Pantheism (all-god) and polytheism (many gods) are actually variations of atheism, since all three systems reject the concept of a true Creator who called the universe itself into existence.

The two competing world views can also be called creationism and evolutionism. Any system rejecting an omnipotent Creator identifies the universe and its processes as sufficient in themselves. These processes are "natural" processes, whereas processes of true creation (i.e., calling something into existence out of nothing but the power of the Creator) by definition must be supernatural. Thus, natural processes of origin and development of complex systems, including living systems, are called evolutionary processes, whereas true creation presumes supernatural processes.

Many philosophies and religions are built around evolutionary humanism, and various religious systems are based on theistic creationism; these are the two basic world views. This choice, therefore, is logically the first decision that should be made by one seriously seeking the truth about life and its meaning.

The Necessity of Faith

This decision should be based on careful consideration of the evidence, but in the end it must be made by faith. It is misleading for people to claim that creationism is based on faith whereas evolutionism is based on science. As we shall see later in detail, it requires much greater faith to believe in evolution than in creation, for the evolutionist must believe that natural processes operating with no intelligent direction—that is, by chance—can generate complex functioning systems out of random particles. No one ever sees any such thing happening in the real world.

The atheist, on the other hand, lodges certain objections against theism. "How can a God who is both omnipotent and caring be reconciled with the existence of so much evil in the world? Either he doesn't care, or he is unable to correct it. Neither alternative supports the assumption that there is really a God who created these things."

In any case, this is a vitally important choice which everyone must make eventually. It is a choice which will affect one's whole life and eternal future, for good or ill, so he needs to consider it carefully. He cannot depend merely on the testimony of others because there have been many brilliant men who were theistic creationists (Isaac Newton, Louis Pasteur, C. S. Lewis, Thomas Jefferson) and many who were atheistic evolutionists (Thomas Huxley, Isaac Asimov, Karl Marx, Sigmund Freud).

I hope to persuade you that the best and most rational choice is that of true monotheism and true creationism. However, no creationist can prove his position, any more than the atheist can prove his atheism; all must ultimately choose for themselves which is the more reasonable faith. Then they must exercise their own wills to make that choice and commit their lives to it.

The Atheistic Faith of Evolution

Many evolutionists deny that they are atheists, but the fact is that evolution itself is atheistic. Although not all evolutionists are atheists, all atheists believe in evolution. The very purpose of evolutionary theory is to explain the origin and development of all things naturalistically. And if evolution is the true explanation of life, God is redundant.

As Sir Julian Huxley said in his keynote address to the assembled intellectuals at the 1959 Darwinian Centennial Convocation in Chicago: "Darwinism removed the whole idea of God as the creator of organisms from the sphere of rational discussion. Darwin pointed out that no supernatural designer was needed: since natural selection could account for any known form of life, there was no room for a supernatural agency in its evolution."[1]

The logic of this statement is unassailable if it is really true that natural selection, or any form of evolution, can account for all forms of life. That, however, is the question.

Life and the Laws of Probability

Human experience proves that buildings, machines, and other complex systems do not originate by chance; they must be designed by an intelligent planner and constructed by careful craftsmen. Yet evolutionists blithely assume that the infinitely complex universe and all the highly organized living systems on the earth somehow came about by time and chance, by purely natural processes operating without intelligent guidance. The omnipotence attributed by Huxley to natural selection is set forth in the following remarkable quotation.

"One with three million noughts after it is the measure of the unlikeliness of a horse—the odds against it happening at all. No one would bet on anything so improbable happening: *and yet it has happened*! It has happened, thanks to the working of natural selection and the properties of living substance which make natural selection inevitable."[2]

Huxley, in making this calculation, assumed that a million favorable mutations would be required to develop a horse from the first primitive cell. Actually, it would be considerably more than this, for a horse consists of far more than a million integrated, functioning cellular components, each of which would require either careful design or a remarkable accident to fit into all the rest. Furthermore, Huxley assumed that one out of every thousand mutations would be beneficial; in reality it would be far less than this, since no one even yet has documented one truly beneficial mutation of anything! Thus he grossly overestimated the probability that a horse could arise as a fortuitous combination of favorable mutations. The probability by any rational application of the principles of mathematics is absolute zero!

Yet Huxley assumed that natural selection had accomplished this miracle. He believed that during the geological ages enough favorable mutations had been preserved by natural selection, each one latching on to the previous one, to generate a horse from this primordial cell. Similar reasoning was applied to the evolution of every other species of plant or animal from that same primitive cell.

This kind of reasoning is not science; it is belief in magic. The good fairy can transform a frog into a prince and natural selection can transform an amoeba into a man! Darwinism did not "remove the idea of God from the sphere of rational discussion," as Huxley alleged; it removed rational discussion from so-called evolutionary science by insisting that organized working systems can arise by chance.

Even the simple primordial cell could not have come together by chance. Sir Francis Crick, one of the discoverers of DNA, the remarkable molecule that carries the coding for reproduction of all forms of life, certainly understands the nature of living substance as well as any man living; and being an atheist, he believes thoroughly in naturalistic evolution. Yet when he calculated the probability of chance origin of even a simple protein sequence of just two hundred amino acids, far simpler than a DNA molecule, he found it to be one chance out of a number approximately equal to 10^{260}; that is, a 1 followed by 260 zeroes.[3] He therefore concluded: "An honest man, armed with all the knowledge available to us now, could only state that in some sense, the origin of life appears at the moment to be almost a miracle, so many are the conditions which would have had to have been satisfied to get it going."[4]

Sir Francis had to call it "almost a miracle," since he does not believe in miracles. However, he then resorted to an even more unlikely solution: the idea that these first living forms originated elsewhere in the universe and were somehow translated to earth. He calls this imaginary process "directed panspermia", and it is sheer speculation. No scientific evidence whatever exists for life anywhere in the universe except on earth. It is merely a desperate attempt to escape the conclusion that life was supernaturally created.

When evolutionists are confronted with this type of argument, however, they commonly respond by saying that even these infinitesimal probabilities are the same as for any other chance combinations. If some other arrangement had come along, then evolution might have proceeded in some other direction, they say.

Such an answer completely begs the question, since only an exceedingly small number of arrangements of any given set of components in a system, as compared to the total number of possible arrangements of those components, would contain information organized to specify any kind of activity at all—let alone evolution.

Molecular biologist Hubert P. Yockey says: "A practical man will not believe a scenario which appears to him to have a very small probability...if a tossed coin is observed to fall heads ten times consecutively, a practical man will believe it to be two-headed without examining it, even though the sequence of all heads is exactly as probable as any other sequence."[5]

Thus, even though Yockey is himself an evolutionist, he recognizes that the evolutionary origin of life at even the simplest level is without evidence. "One must conclude that, contrary to the established and current wisdom, a scenario describing the genesis of life on earth by chance and natural causes which can be accepted on the basis of fact and not faith has not yet been written."[6]

The Mystery of Evolution

Julian Huxley was confident that natural selection, acting on randomly produced beneficial mutations, could overcome the vast improbabilities implied in the chance origin of instant complexity. A present-day neo-Darwinist, Richard Dawkins, still defends the same notion: "Complexity cannot spring up in a single stroke of chance: that would be like hitting upon the combination number that opens a bank vault. But a whole series of tiny chance steps, if non-randomly selected, can build up almost limitless complexity of adaptation. It is as though the vault's door were to open another chink every time the number on the dials moved a little closer to the winning number."[7]

But bank vaults don't work this way, and neither does evolution. Mutations do not produce increased complexity, and natural selection cannot preserve increased complexity which is never presented to it. That is why no one has ever observed real evolution taking place.

"No one has ever produced a species by mechanisms of natural selection. No one has ever gotten near it," says Colin Patterson, one of the world's leading evolutionists, who is on the scientific staff of the British Museum of Natural History.[8] Even Charles Darwin really didn't prove that the origin of new species occurs by natural selection. "As Ernst Mayr, one of the founders of the

modern synthetic theory of evolution, pointed out. . .
Darwin never really did discuss the origin of the species
in his *On the Origin of Species*."[9]

Natural selection is not the omnipotent creator that
Darwin, Huxley, Dawkins, and others have believed it to
be. Pierre Grassè, who as one of the world's leading zoolo-
gists held the Chair of Evolution at the Sorbonne in Paris
for over thirty years, said: "The opportune appearance of
mutations permitting animals and plants to meet their
needs seems hard to believe. Yet the Darwinian theory is
even more demanding. A single plant, a single animal
would require thousands and thousands of lucky, appropriate events. Thus miracles would become the rule:
events with an infinitesimal probability could not fail to
occur. . . . There is no law against daydreaming, but science must not indulge in it."[10]

Grassè was not arguing against evolution, of course;
but he did recognize that chance and natural selection
could not do it. "Directed by all-powerful selection,
chance becomes a sort of providence, which, under the
cover of atheism, is not named but is secretly worshipped."[11]

In short, there is a growing recognition among modern
evolutionists that atheistic evolutionism, operating ma-
terialistically by chance and natural selection, does not
work. A number of modern theories have been proposed
for evolution's mechanism (among them, punctuated
equilibrium, genetic drift, and acquired characteristics),
but no proof has been forthcoming for any of them.

"Today we are less confident and the whole subject is
in the most exciting ferment. Evolution is both troubled
from without by the nagging insistence of anti-scientists
and nagged from within by the troubling complexities of
genetic and developmental mechanisms and new questions about the central mystery—speciation itself," says
Keith Stewart Thomson, professor of biology and dean of
the graduate school at Yale University.[12] This is a fas-

cinating admission! A century and a quarter after Darwin was supposed to have solved this problem, the mechanism for the evolution of new species is still the central mystery.

One wonders how evolutionists can be so sure evolution is true when they don't know how it works and have never seen it produce even one new species, let alone new genera and families and life itself. It should be obvious that evolutionary atheism (or humanism, materialism, or whatever one calls it) is held strictly by faith. It is the religion of Marxism and all other atheistic belief systems, but it is not science!

Probably the most prolific scientist living today is Isaac Asimov, author of approximately three hundred books on just about every field of science. He is an avowed atheist and current (1988) president of the American Humanist Association. If anyone living is familiar with the whole field of modern science, it is Asimov. Yet he admits: "I don't have the evidence to prove that God doesn't exist."[13]

The fact is, there is no scientific evidence for naturalistic evolution. The god of atheism—time and chance—is unable to create anything but decay and death.

2

The Immoral Gods of Pantheism

Although the leaders of evolutionary thought in the Western world are still largely committed to an atheistic approach—either the gradualism of neo-Darwinism or the punctuationism of Marxist dialectics—there is an increasing interest today in some form of pantheistic evolution. Strict materialism has proved barren both spiritually and scientifically. Time and chance, random mutation, and natural selection never develop higher organisms from lower, as stressed in the preceding chapter. Consequently, many European and American scientists are turning to some form of "creative evolution," guided by supposed mystical principles innate in the cosmos.

This is nothing new in the East, of course. All of the Eastern religions have developed around some form of pantheistic evolution and so have adapted easily to the modern evolutionary world view. While such pantheistic ideas may seem at first to mediate between naturalistic evolutionism and supernaturalistic creationism, the fact is that they are only varieties of evolution.

23

Evolutionary Religions

All the great religions of the world, both ancient and modern, are fundamentally evolutionary pantheism. That is, all of them assume an eternal cosmos and deny a transcendent creator. Consider the ancient religions of China, for example.

One authority says: "In contrast to the Western world, the Far Eastern philosophers thought of creation in evolutionary terms. . . . The striking feature of the Chinese concept of cosmogony is the fact that creation was never associated with the design or activity of a supernatural being, but rather with the interaction of impersonal forces, the powers of which persist interminably."[1]

Michael Ruse, a leading philosopher and historian of evolutionism, makes the following interesting analysis of Chinese communism, while reviewing a recent book on evolutionism in China: "[Darwin's] ideas took root at once, for China did not have the innate intellectual and religious barriers to evolution that often existed in the West. Indeed, in some respects Darwin seemed almost Chinese!. . . Taoist and neo-Confucian thought had always stressed the 'thingness' of humans. Our being at one with the animals was no great shock."[2]

Buddhism, Hinduism, Shintoism, Lamaism, Jainism, and Sikhism are also pantheistic religions, along with other more modern forms of Eastern mysticism. The ancient religions of Egypt, Babylonia, and Europe were variations on the same themes.

"Even some primitive mythologies express the idea that life in all its diverse manifestations is not the creation of the gods but a purely natural phenomenon being the result of normal flux of the world. The ancient Norse, for example, held that the first living beings, the giant Ymir and the primordial cow Audumla, were formed gradually from the ice melted by the action of the warm wind which blew from a southern land Myspell-sheim, the land of fire."[3]

The pagan religions of ancient Greece and Rome provide further examples: "The majority of the old pre-Socratic philosophers were strikingly materialistic in their interpretation of nature. To them life was a natural phenomenon, the result of processes no less natural than those which molded the forms of rocks or rivers, no less inevitable than the turn of the tides, the phases of the moon. Life was for them part of a continuum with the soil and sea."[4]

The numerous gods and goddesses of the official pantheon, visualized in images everywhere on the streets and in the temples, personified various natural forces and systems (e.g. the god of fire, the goddess of the river), each being merely one aspect of the great "all-god" who was equivalent to the universe itself.

Associated with each ancient ethnic religion and its complex of pantheism and polytheism, there was usually a belief in astrology and spiritism, and this is still true today. To a considerable extent, the various star images in the heavens correspond with the gods and goddesses in the pantheon, and the spirits are considered to be either those of ancestors or of demons. In any case, all things, living or non-living, are believed to be products of the innate processes and systems of the eternally changing universe.

New Age Religions

Many of these ancient pantheistic religions are undergoing a remarkable revival today in both East and West. In the West they are to considerable extent joining up with certain avant-garde scientific concepts in a complex of organizations, philosophies, and practices often called the New Age movement.

Recent statements by Harvard professor George Wald, former Nobel Prize winner previously regarded by most intellectuals as an atheistic evolutionist, point out the pantheistic flavor of this movement.

"Perhaps consciousness, rather than being a late evolutionary development, was there all the time. Consciousness formed the material universe and brought out life and overt forms of consciousness.... The universe wants to be known. Did the universe come about to play its role to empty benches?"[5]

Such ideas do not imply, however, that Wald is returning to creationism or biblical orthodoxy. His concept of a conscious universe is not that of a personal Creator but the impersonal cosmic mind of the ancient pantheist, immanent in nature rather than transcendent to it.

The "anthropic principle," currently enjoying great popularity among top-flight physicists and other scientists, is used to stress the remarkable correlation of cosmic constants with the existence of human life on earth and then to draw the same dubious conclusion. "At the least the anthropic principle suggests connections between the existence of man and aspects of physics that one might have thought would have little bearing on biology. In its strongest form the principle might reveal that the universe we live in is the only conceivable universe in which intelligent life could exist."[6]

A New Age journalist describes this anthropic principle in the following terms: "The window of initial conditions necessary to produce our kind is very narrow, it turns out.... Given the facts, our existence seems quite improbable—more miraculous, perhaps, than the seven-day wonder of Genesis. As physicist Freeman Dyson of the Institute for Advanced Study in Princeton, New Jersey, once remarked, 'The universe in some sense must have known we were coming.'"[7]

The connection between advanced cosmo-physics, evo-lutionary biology, and eastern mysticism has been dis-cussed in some detail by University of California physicist Fritjof Capra, whose writings are much admired by most New Agers. Dr. Capra stresses what he calls "systems biology," the idea that organisms cannot be understood except as components of a hierarchy of nested ecosystems, with the whole world ultimately comprising a giant ecosystem interacting with all its parts, the whole thereby becoming in effect a living organism in itself (*Gaia*, it is called, or even Mother Nature). An invisible biological field supposedly emanates from each organism and each ecosystem in turn, like the force field surround-ing a magnet. This powerful complex of fields controls and directs the universal process of evolution, propelling the world toward ever-higher levels of self-organization.

Capra says: "The new systems biology shows that fluc-tuations are crucial in the dynamics of self-organization. They are the basis of order in the living world: ordered structures arise from rhythmic patterns. . . ." "The idea of fluctuations as the basis of order, which Nobel laureate Ilya Prigogine introduced into modern science, is one of the major themes in all Taoist texts. The mutual inter-dependence of all aspects of reality and the non-linear nature of its interconnections are emphasized throughout Eastern mysticism."[8]

The weak scientific evidence for this notion of self-organization through rhythmic fluctuations will be dis-cussed in the next chapter. The significant point here, however, is that all pantheistic systems, whether ancient Taoism, Buddhism, Hinduism, or modern New Ageism, are supposed to provide the forces of evolution by means of the power and intelligence of the universe itself. What the god of chance and atheistic materialism cannot achieve, Mother Nature and her earth-energy can do, so they believe. "Evolution is no longer viewed as a mindless affair; quite the opposite. It is mind enlarging its domain up the chain of species."[9]

The patron saint of the modern New Age movement is the controversial Jesuit priest Teilhard de Chardin, French theologian and paleontologist. To him, evolution itself was god.

"[Evolution] is a general postulate to which all theories, all hypotheses, all systems must henceforward bow and which they must satisfy in order to be thinkable and true. Evolution is a light which illuminates all facts, a trajectory which all lines of thought must follow."[10]

This tribute to the great god evolution was cited by geneticist Francisco Ayala in his obituary tribute to Theodosius Dobzhansky, a disciple of Teilhard de Chardin. Dobzhansky was one of the leaders of the neo-Darwinian mechanistic theory of evolution, but could himself be considered an early New Ager.

Speaking of him, Ayala said: "Dobzhansky was a religious man, although he apparently rejected fundamental beliefs of traditional religion, such as the existence of a personal God and of life beyond physical death.... Dobzhansky held that, in man, biological evolution has transcended itself into the realm of self-awareness and culture. He believed that mankind would eventually evolve into higher levels of harmony and creativity. He was a metaphysical optimist."[11]

In fact, Ayala called Dobzhansky "perhaps the most eminent evolutionist of the twentieth century,"[12] and there is no doubt that more and more modern evolutionary scientists are also becoming pantheists.

This is not to say, of course, that these scientists necessarily partake of all other aspects of the New Age movement, which embraces groups and beliefs of all sorts—meditationists, astrologists, parapsychologists, health-faddists, and others. Numerous quasi-Christian sects are involved also—Unity, Divine Science—not to mention religious cults such as the Rosicrucians and Theosophists, as well as the many Eastern religions—Hare Krishna, Zen Buddhism—that have become prominent in recent years.

As diverse as these groups may be, they still agree on certain key essentials which, in effect, make them one great movement. All are committed to some form of pantheistic evolution, to some form of humanism, and to some form of globalism, promoting a future world government and world religion. Jeremy Rifkin has expressed the philosophy of the movement in the following pungent words.

"We no longer feel ourselves to be guests in someone else's home and therefore obliged to make our behavior conform with a set of pre-existing cosmic rules. It is our creation now. We make the rules. We establish the parameters of reality. We create the world, and because we do, we no longer feel beholden to outside forces. We no longer have to justify our behavior, for we are now the architects of the universe. We are responsible to nothing outside ourselves, for we are the kingdom, the power, and the glory for ever and ever."[13]

May the force be with us!

Moral Implications of Evolutionary Pantheism

The great advantage of pantheism over atheism is that it professes to add the dimension of "mind" to raw chance as the agency of evolution. However, the addition of a mental factor implies a moral factor. If blind chance operates in such a way as to produce inequities or sufferings or deaths, no one feels any kind of moral reaction against it, because chance can make no distinction between right and wrong. If conscious direction is involved, then the morality of the planner becomes a factor. However, right and wrong may in this case be defined quite differently than in the case of special creation by an omnipotent Creator.

That is, if evolution (or nature or cosmic mind or the force) is, in effect, deified, then whatever advances evolution becomes right and moral. When Sir Julian Huxley, the world's leading evolutionist at the time, was chosen to be UNESCO's first Director General, his goal was the establishment of a worldwide humanistic religion and world government, both of which would be speeded up by man-controlled evolution.

In his article, "A New World Vision," which constituted Huxley's originally proposed Framework for UNESCO when it was established following World War II, he stated: "Thus the general philosophy of UNESCO should, it seems, be a scientific world humanism, global in extent and evolutionary in background. . . . From the evolutionary point of view, the destiny of man may be summed up very simply: it is to realize the maximum progress in the minimum time."[14]

According to Huxley's Framework, the standards of morality would no longer be the traditional code of conduct based on God's Ten Commandments, but rather on what would best promote genetic, social, cultural, and economic evolution. "The analysis of evolutionary progress gives us certain criteria for judging the rightness or wrongness of our aims or activities and the desirability, or otherwise, of the tendencies to be noted in contemporary history."[15]

The great problem with any such criteria, of course, is that they must be based on what the power elite decide are the desirable evolutionary goals. This determines what type of government and religion should be established and which political and social policies should be implemented to attain them. Some may decide on Fascism, some on Communism, some on a utopian democracy. The world religion will necessarily be some form of humanism or mysticism or both. In any case, unification must be achieved, and all dissent suppressed.

"The unifying of traditions into a single common pool of experience, awareness, and purpose is the necessary prerequisite for further major progress in human evolution. Accordingly, although political unification in some sort of world government will be required for the definitive attainment of this stage, unification in the things of the mind is not only necessary also, but it can pave the way for other types of unification."[16]

Huxley had in mind a world government of socialism and a world religion of humanism, as have most of his followers in UNESCO and the United Nations. These goals are also set forth in the "Tenets of Humanism" which he, along with John Dewey and other leaders of like mind, helped to formulate for the American Humanist Association when it was set up back in 1933. Most of the leaders in our modern scientific and educational establishments, as well as practically all New Age organizations, still look toward such goals. This is the underlying reason for their intense and emotional opposition to the modern creationist movement which seeks to restore commitment to the true God of creation.

The morality of evolutionary pantheism is altogether conditioned by such goals. Whatever contributes to the attainment of the evolutionary goal—even the starvation of millions of Ukrainian farmers in the cause of Russian Communism or the genocide of the Jewish race as in German Nazism—is thereby moral and right.

The unspeakable ravages of the Nazis and the horrifying atrocities of the Russian and Chinese communists constitute an eloquent commentary on the true morality of evolutionary pantheism, for Hitler and Marx and their followers were evolutionary pantheists in the fullest sense. Adolf Hitler came into power pretending to be Roman Catholic but was really a devotee of occultism and desired to restore the religion of the ancient Teutonic gods. He was also passionately devoted to evolutionism and was a committed follower of Nietzsche, Haeckel, and Darwin.

It is commonly believed that Karl Marx was an atheist, but actually he was a pantheist. (In a very real sense, as already noted, pantheism is nothing but atheism made more potent by a pseudopurposiveness and pseudomorality.) Richard Wurmbrand, who has himself suffered much under Communism and has devoted his life to a study of its evil background and policies for the future, has provided extensive documentation to show that Marx also was an occultist and even a Satanist.[17] According to Wurmbrand, the same is true of Lenin, Stalin, and other communist leaders.

Thus, whereas atheistic evolutionism is impotent and incapable of mechanistically generating complex systems, pantheistic evolutionism must face the even more serious charge of cruelty and immorality in its professedly more goal-oriented development of the world and its creatures.

Theistic Evolution

At this point it is necessary to say a few words about the belief known as theistic evolution. Held by many monotheists—people who believe in a personal Creator God, such as Christians, Jews, and Muslims—this idea maintains that God actually created the world, but that he did so by the process of evolution.

This is not only completely contrary to the teachings of the Bible, but is also completely incompatible with an omniscient, merciful God. Evolution is a wasteful, inefficient, and cruel process. Surely an omnipotent God could devise a better plan than this. Most importantly, a God of love and grace could never be guilty of imposing such a monstrously sadistic system on his living creatures.

It is little wonder, then, that capitulation to evolutionism has led to so many evil philosophies and practices, even in the "Christianized" world of Europe and America. Kenneth Hsu, an evolutionary geologist, recently commented: "Darwinism was also used in a defense of competitive individualism and its economic corollary of laissez-faire capitalism in England and in America. Andrew Carnegie wrote that the 'law of competition, be it benign or not, is here; we cannot evade it.' Rockefeller went a step further when he claimed that the 'growth of a large business is merely a survival of the fittest; it is merely the working out of a law of nature and a law of God.'

"Not only capitalists but also socialists welcomed Darwinism; Karl Marx thought Darwin's book important because it supported the class struggle in history from the point of view of natural science. Worst of all, Darwinism opened the door to racists who wanted to apply the principle of natural selection to better mankind. Darwin's theory in biology, transferred to Germany and nurtured by Ernst Haeckel, inspired an ideology that led eventually to the rise of the Nazis."[18]

Hsu was criticizing Darwinism, of course, not evolutionism as such. Hsu himself is an advocate of the saltational school of evolutionary thought, which stresses punctuationism and extinctionism in biology and catastrophism in geology.

Whatever view of evolution one holds, the fact remains that its supposed billion-year spectacle of suffering and death, as recorded in the fossil beds of the sedimentary rocks of the earth's crust, is a graphic indictment against any god who would be guilty of such a thing! Nevertheless, evolutionism now dominates the intellectual world and, in its pantheistic, New Age, computer-implemented format, seems to be growing stronger all the time.

Socialist Jeremy Rifkin, though himself an evolutionist, considers it inevitable that evolutionary pantheism will soon unite the whole world in its politico-religious grip, and that this will be the greatest calamity in history. He concludes his remarkable book on algeny with the ominous words: "Our future is secured. The cosmos wails."[19]

3

Science and the God of Creation

In the two preceding chapters outlining some of the evidence against evolution, we have seen that neither the materialistic god of the atheist nor the mystical god of the pantheist can really serve as the explanation for the origin and evolution of the cosmos. The first is utterly impotent to produce a complex universe, for chance and natural selection can never generate organized, functioning systems. The second is based solely on speculative metaphysics and, even if really capable of conscious direction, is utterly amoral. In terms of scientific evidence, evolution is utterly mysterious as to mechanism since it is never observed in action. When applied philosophically in human societies, it is deadly.

The only other alternative, therefore, is the living, personal, omnipotent, holy God of creation. Evolutionists, both atheistic and pantheistic, have always vigorously denounced belief in a personal, omnipotent God as unscientific, but the truth is that all the facts of the real world conform perfectly to the existence and creative work of a supernatural Creator.

The Living World

The living world with its array of distinctive plants and animals, each with a complex, intricate structure designed to serve ordained purposes, is exactly what one would expect of an omniscient Creator. Even Harvard's preeminent Stephen Jay Gould, an atheist, recognizes this: "In fact, as Darwin recognized, a perfect Creator could manufacture perfect adaptations. Everything would fit because everything was designed to fit."[1] Gould even argues that it is only the imperfections in plants and animals that argue against creation and for evolution. "It is in the imperfect adaptations that natural selection is revealed, because it is those imperfections that show us that a structure has a history. If there were no imperfections, there would be no evidence of history, and therefore nothing to favor evolution by natural selection over creation."[2]

This is strange reasoning. Why assume that a primevally perfect creation must always continue in a state of perfection? In fact, as we shall see shortly, one of the strong evidences of creation is the universal law of disintegration known as the law of entropy. Nevertheless, for a man like Gould, who is the top evolutionist today—or at least the most articulate—to say that the only real evidence for evolution is found in the few "imperfections" that may exist in nature is an amazing admission of the bankruptcy of evolutionary thought.

On the other hand, the exquisite and intricate perfection of all organisms in relation to their environments is exactly what would be expected if they had been specially created. Furthermore, the great variety of individual characteristics within each kind of creature (no two individuals are exactly alike), in relation to the clear-cut gaps between the kinds (e.g., the many varieties of dogs and cats, with no intermediates between dogs and cats) is, again, exactly what would be expected of an intelligent and gracious Creator. If some process of evolution had produced all these kinds of organisms from some "nested hierarchy" of common ancestors, then a more reasonable expectation would have been a "continuum" between all the kinds, as well as a continuing "evolutionary flux" between them.

"The fact that so many of the founders of modern biology, those who discovered all the basic facts of comparative morphology upon which modern evolutionary biology is based, held nature to be fundamentally a discontinuum of isolated and unique types unbridged by transitional varieties, a position absolutely at odds with evolutionary ideas, is obviously very difficult to reconcile with the popular notion that all the facts of biology irrefutably support an evolutionary interpretation."[3]

Thus, as far as existing plants and animals are concerned, the data fit beautifully with the premise of original special creation rather than evolution. What we see in the living world is exactly what the creationist would expect to be there: many distinct "kinds" of organisms, with much horizontal variation (at the same level of complexity) within the kinds, but clear and unbridgeable gaps between the kinds. Whenever "vertical changes" do occur, they are never upward toward higher levels of organization; they are always downward—imperfections, mutations, death, sometimes even extinction, exactly the reverse of what true evolution should require. All of this is strong and clear scientific evidence for primeval creation.

The Fossil World

The same testimony is given by the fossil record. Billions of fossil remains of formerly living creatures have been preserved in the sedimentary rocks of the earth's crust. Tens of millions of these have actually been catalogued for collections in museums and other places. Although fossils normally preserve only the hard parts of the organisms, such as shells and bones, these are so numerous that they have given a reasonable picture of the life of earlier times.

The fossil record reveals the same types of phenomena as the living world; that is, horizontal changes within limits and unbridged gaps between the basic kinds. Although many fossilized animals are now extinct (e.g., dinosaurs), out of the billions of fossils, there are no true transitional forms. This also is more compatible with creationist concepts than with evolutionary theory.

The fact that there are no real transitional forms in the fossil record is confirmed by several leading paleontologists. Dr. Tom Kemp, curator of the Oxford University Museum, says: "As is now well known, most fossil species appear instantaneously in the record, persist for some millions of years virtually unchanged, only to disappear abruptly—the 'punctuated equilibrium' pattern of Eldredge and Gould."[4] And Dr. Steven Stanley, professor of paleontology at Johns Hopkins, attests: "The known fossil record fails to document a single example of phyletic evolution accomplishing a major morphologic transition."[5]

Even Dr. Gould admits that "The absence of fossil evidence for intermediary stages between major transitions in organic design, indeed our inability, even in our imagination, to construct functional intermediates in many cases, has been a persistent and nagging problem for gradualistic accounts of evolution."[6]

Evolutionists, especially Charles Darwin, used to attribute the absence of transitional fossils to the incompleteness of the fossil record, but this explanation is impossibly naive. As Denton says: "Since Darwin's time the search for missing links in the fossil record has continued on an ever-increasing scale. So vast has been the expansion of paleontological activity over the past one hundred years that probably 99.9% of all paleontological work has been carried out since 1860. Only a small fraction of the hundred thousand or so fossil species known today were known to Darwin. But virtually all the new fossil species discovered since Darwin's time have either been closely related to known forms or, like the Poganophoras, strange unique types of unknown affinity."[7]

It is true that evolutionists cite a few fossils as possible transitional forms, notably *Archaeopteryx*, the supposed reptile/bird, along with the so-called mammal-like reptiles and the famous horse series. These, however, are not evolutionary transitions at all, despite the wishful thinking of evolutionists.

At best, *Archaeopteryx* and the mammal-like reptiles are "mosaic" forms. That is, each such animal possessed a mosaic of structures which were all fully developed and perfectly functional. Gould and Eldredge have acknowledged that "there is certainly no evidence for [intermediates] in the fossil record (curious mosaics like *Archaeopteryx* do not count)."[8]

A real transitional form would show structures or organs in the process of changing (e.g., scales becoming feathers, legs becoming wings, half-developed hearts), but animals with such useless appendages would not even survive to evolve into some more viable form.

The case for *Archaeopteryx* as the ancestral bird was weakened still further by the discovery of two fossil birds (true birds, not intermediates) in strata dated older than *Archaeopteryx*. Finally, a strong case has recently been made by several scientists that the only two significant fossils of this creature were actually the product of an audacious hoax perpetrated shortly after Darwin's book had been published in 1859. (This controversial charge has been indignantly rejected by orthodox evolutionists, but Hoyle in turn has rebutted their own counter argument. The fossils are at least open to question.)[9]

The mammal-like reptiles are even less defensible as candidates for transitional animals. Dr. Denton points out: "The possibility that the mammal-like reptiles were completely reptilian in terms of their anatomy and physiology cannot be excluded. The only evidence we have regarding their soft biology is their cranial endocasts and these suggest that, as far as their central nervous systems were concerned, they were entirely reptilian."[10]

There were many genera of these mammal-like reptiles, but all are extinct and unavailable for study in the flesh. The skeletons of modern reptiles and mammals can be differentiated only on the basis of certain bones associated with hearing and chewing, yet the two classes are grossly different in other aspects which cannot be preserved as fossils. Furthermore, each individual kind of these extinct creatures was completely different from any other animal, with no transitional forms anywhere.

Kemp, one of the top authorities on mammal-like reptiles confirms this: "Each species of mammal-like reptile that has been found appears suddenly in the fossil record and is not preceded by the species that is directly ancestral to it. It disappears some time later, without leaving a directly descended species."[11]

The same is true with the fossil horses, which no longer are considered to represent a family tree, ascending linearly from the dawn horse to the modern horse. "It's a very bushy sort of pattern that is, I think, much more in line with the punctuational model; there isn't just a simple gradual transition from one horse to another."[12]

There are no candidates for transition from the invertebrates to the vertebrates, nor from the protozoa to the invertebrates. The origins of insects, amphibians, and reptiles are utterly undocumented. Each order of mammals appears suddenly and fully developed in the fossil record, without antecedents or interconnections. The assumed ancestry of man is so confused that many anthropologists now argue that the apes may have descended from a man-like ancestor!

So many mistakes of interpretation (not to mention hoaxes) have plagued paleontologists that the whole subject of the fossil record has inspired the following evaluation from evolutionist Jeremy Rifkin: "What the 'record' shows is nearly a century of fudging and finagling by scientists to conform with Darwin's notions, all to no avail. Today the millions of fossils stand as very visible, ever-present reminders of the paltriness of the arguments and the overall shabbiness of the theory that marches under the banner of evolution."[13]

No wonder Mark Ridley, eminent Oxford zoologist, even while trying to defend evolution against creationists, was forced to conclude: "In any case, no real evolutionist, whether gradualist or punctuationist, uses the fossil record as evidence in favor of the theory of evolution as opposed to special creation."[14]

Yet this same fossil record, which is an embarrassment to evolutionists, yields strong evidence for special creation, with each kind of organism complete, recognizable, fully developed and functional the very first time it appears in the record.

The Possible World

One of the strongest evidences of the God of Creation is the nature of the two fundamental laws of science which are now known to govern all processes in our world: the first and second laws of thermodynamics. No evidence of evolution is ever seen either in the living world or in the fossil world because these basic laws preclude it.

The first law, also called the law of conservation of mass/energy, states that the totality of mass-plus-energy is always "conserved" in any isolated system, neither being created nor annihilated. Since everything is either energy or mass, and since the whole universe can be considered as an isolated system, this law states that nothing is being "created" by present natural processes, all of which must—by definition—obey this basic natural law. All that exists, therefore, must have been created at some point in the past by processes not operational in the present at all.

The second law, also called the law of increasing entropy, states that entropy (which is, essentially, a measure of disorganization) always increases in any isolated functioning system. That is, engines run down, materials wear out, structures disintegrate, and organisms grow old and die. Everything, so to speak, was "wound up" sometime in the past and is now running down, like a great cosmic clock.

These two basic laws of science are the best-proved, most universally applicable laws known to scientists. No exception to either has ever been observed, except in the case of true miracles.

Now, note how these two laws testify to the primeval special, miraculous, creation of the universe and all its complex systems, including its living creatures. The second law requires that the universe must somehow have been created in the past because it is running down in the present. The first law states that the universe could not have created itself, since nothing in the processes of the universe can now create anything. If it must have been created, but could not have created itself, then it must have been created by a creator external to itself, a creator capable of designing a complex cosmos.

The principle of causality—that is, that every effect must have an adequate cause—is the fundamental premise of all sound science. The relating of effects to their causes is the goal of all scientific research, and there is no reason not to apply the principle to the universe itself. Thus, the creator of the universe, the great uncaused First Cause of all things, must be capable of calling into existence the infinite, eternal cosmos with all its beauty, complexity, life, and love. By the law of cause and effect, therefore, the cause and creator of the universe must be an infinite, eternal, omnipotent, omniscient, living, loving Being! This can be none other than the one, personal, transcendent God of all creation.

Unfortunately, people through the ages have sought by many devices to escape the testimony of special creation, inventing a wide assortment of evolutionary theories to try to explain the universe without a real Creator God. It is a remarkable testimony to human perversity that in our modern scientific age, when the best established and most basic principles of science point directly to the Creator, the scientific establishment still commits itself to the philosophy of evolutionary humanism. The big bang theory (that is, that the universe originated billions of years ago in a single explosion of energy) directly contradicts the second law of thermodynamics; yet evolutionists persist in believing it. Some, like Richard Morris, at least recognize the problem.

"Presumably the universe began in a very chaotic state. A chaotic state is, by definition, a state of high entropy (when we speak of 'chaos,' we mean that there is a great deal of disorder). On the other hand, numerous kinds of structure have appeared since the universe began. For example, stars and galaxies have formed. The creation of this structure, and the fact that stars gain entropy as they burn their nuclear fuel, would seem to imply that the universe is far from a state of maximum entropy now. But how can this be, if entropy was so high at the beginning? Doesn't the second law of thermodynamics tell us that entropy always increased with time?"[15]

Evolutionary cosmogonists commonly attempt to bypass this fundamental problem by assuming that the state of the universe immediately following the big bang was one of exceedingly high order. This is absurd. Explosions produce disorder, and the supposed big bang would have been the greatest of all explosions! Furthermore, it presumably generated only hydrogen atoms—the simplest of all atoms—at the start, and to think that hydrogen gas could somehow evolve into all the other elements and then into stars and planets and people is sheer fantasy.

In any case, it is obvious that creationism is in exact agreement with the two laws. In fact, a creationist would predict these laws directly from the assumptions and principles of creationism. That is, one would expect the Creator to impose a principle of conservation upon his perfect creation in order to preserve its basic nature. One would also expect a second principle of qualitative change and variation to supplement the basic principle of quantitative stability. Any such changes could be only horizontal (within limits) or downward, since all organized structures were created perfect and could not be improved. These laws—especially the second—would also serve the purpose of testifying to the necessity of primeval supernatural creation by a transcendent Creator, as discussed above.

In a widely used textbook on thermodynamics, two eminent scientists conclude their discussion of these philosophical implications as follows: "we see the second law of thermodynamics as a description of the prior and continuing work of a creator, who also holds the key to our future destiny and that of the universe."[16]

It should be crystal clear that, at least as far as the universe as a whole is concerned, the basic laws of science constitute an irrefutable evidence that it was created supernaturally by a transcendent and omnipotent Creator.

Entropy versus Evolution

The second law of thermodynamics not only points to the primeval creation of the universe, but also refutes upward evolution at every level. The entropy principle is valid for every kind of system, large or small, physical or biological. Entropy says, in effect, that every system inherently tends to decay from high organization and complexity. Evolution, on the other hand, implies an innate tendency in nature to generate higher levels of organized complexity. The principles are direct opposites—totally contradictory; they cannot both be true.

The entropy principle, however, is a law of science, whereas evolution is simply a belief system supporting atheistic and pantheistic religions. No one has ever seen anything evolve naturalistically from one kind to a higher kind, but everyone sees the entropy principle in operation all the time. Yet most evolutionists choose to ignore this fundamental conflict.

Those who do respond, usually try to pass it off with the foolish claim that "the entropy law only applies to closed systems, whereas the evolving earth-system is an open system." This is both incorrect and irrelevant. The Second Law applies to all systems, as anyone who is familiar with the equations of thermodynamics knows. That is, an influx of heat energy into an open system (as from the sun onto the earth) will increase the entropy of that system—in fact, increase it more rapidly than if it were a closed system!

Some have tried to bypass the problem by citing the formation of snowflakes or other crystals as examples of natural increases in order, though what this has to do with evolution is a mystery. A snowflake forms when heat energy is *removed* from a water molecular system; yet these evolutionists suggest that this is somehow analogous to the production of evolutionary complexity by the *addition* of heat energy to the earth from the sun. This is strange reasoning.

> The. . . argument that order appears in a cooling body . . . runs against his statement that the flow of heat from the sun to the Earth resulted in photosynthesis and the development of 'highly hierarchical' forms of organic matter on Earth. For one thing, why only Earth? Why has Mars failed the test? And for another, the sun cools and Earth

necessarily warms up (if we consider only the 'sun-Earth system') and therefore it is the sun that should be drawing toward order, Earth toward disorder.[17]

Although most evolutionists have ignored the critical problem of harmonizing evolution with entropy, a few have recognized its significance and tried to find a solution. The most ambitious of these attempts is a recent book which actually tries to equate the two concepts![18]

The authors, Daniel Brooks and E. D. Wiley, argue: "Our theory suggests that evolution is a phenomenon involving systems (species) far from equilibrium. The hierarchy results from speciation, which we will try to show exhibits entropic dynamics analogous to 'ordering through fluctuations.'"[19]

If this seems a bit obscure, consider the following clarification of their theory by these two distinguished biologists: "Why is there order and not chaos in the living world? Because living systems, organisms and species, are individualized dissipative structures (1) exhibiting finite information and cohesion, (2) maintaining themselves through irreversible dissipation of matter and energy, and (3) existing in an open energy system."[20]

Brooks and Wiley elaborate these farfetched ideas with a sophisticated mathematical apparatus and an esoteric philosophical exposition, but the very idea of equating evolution with entropy is like equating east with west, or noon with midnight. There is no need to critique their impossible attempt here; their fellow evolutionists have already done it for us.

Geneticist Joseph Felsenstein of the University of Washington says, for example: "I was disappointed in Brooks' and Wiley's discussion of entropy and evolution because it did not seem to me that they present a theory at all. It is not that their theory is wrong; it seems to be vacuous instead."[21]

This criticism is all the more devastating because Felsenstein realizes the importance of the effort to harmonize evolution with entropy and would like for them to have succeeded.

"Brooks and Wiley have not produced a new evolutionary theory, or even a very useful redescription of existing theories, but I cannot fault them for trying. They see the importance of the task, and here they are right and my fellow population geneticists are both wrong and wrongheaded."[22]

This review of the attempt by Brooks and Wiley to harmonize evolution and entropy was published in the journal of the Society for the Study of Evolution. Published in the same issue was a more extensive and equally critical review by Brian Charlesworth, a biologist at the University of Chicago.

> Their work suffers...from the usual faults of half-baked theorizing in biology. The worst of these is the lack of any convincing derivation of the supposed laws of change from known principles, in contrast to the program of statistical mechanics which provides the background for their ideas....It should be clear that the claim for an inherent evolutionary increase in entropy and organization is based on an arbitrary model which shows signs of having been constructed simply to yield the desired result.[23]

Brooks' and Wiley's detailed study is probably the most serious attempt to harmonize evolution and entropy yet published, but it fails completely. The entropy principle squarely refutes even the possibility of vertically upward evolution. Conversely, it strongly confirms creationist expectations.

All true science supports the God of Creation—the God who is real!

4

The God of the Bible

In earlier chapters we saw that neither the chance evolution of the atheist nor the directed evolution of the pantheist can explain the scientific data related to origins. Furthermore, the social and moral consequences of evolutionism have been disastrous wherever applied.

Therefore, all the real facts of science, as well as the need for stable and beneficial relationships in human societies, ought to lead us to creationism as the true science of origins. Evolutionism—whether the nature worship of ancient pagans or the sophisticated scientism of modern intellectuals—will satisfy neither the data of science nor the spiritual needs of mankind. There must be a God of creation!

But who is this God? Is he the Yahweh of the Hebrews, the Allah of the Arabs, or some Unknown God of Deism? And why did he create the world and us?

Cause and Effect

An excellent way to approach these questions is in terms of the scientific principle of causality. Although some have questioned this principle at the subatomic level, the entire scientific study of the world is built on the premise that effects must be related to causes. No effect can be quantitatively greater or qualitatively distinct from its cause.

Consider the law of cause and effect in relation to the Creator. As the First Cause of the universe, he must be able to create a universe infinite in extent and eternal in duration. This means he also must be both infinite and eternal. Since the infinite space-time universe is everywhere vibrant with force and power, he must have sufficient power to create it all. Thus he must be omnipotent.

Furthermore, since all these energies manifest themselves in an infinite array of complex systems and relationships, each of which must be designed to function properly in its own sphere, he must also be omniscient and omnipresent. And since our world is filled with all kinds of living things, and since life comes only from life, the Creator God must be alive.

Among all these living creatures, the highest are human beings, each of whom is a distinct person with his or her own unique personality, capable of planning, deciding, loving, and recognizing what is true and what is right. The God who created such persons must, by the law of cause and effect, likewise be a person, one who is intelligent, volitional, emotional. The one who created love must be loving, the one who established truth and righteousness must be true and righteous altogether.

Thus, as noted in the preceding chapter, the God of creation is (if causality is a valid principle of reasoning, as it is in all other realms of science and experience) an infinite, eternal, omnipotent, omnipresent, omniscient, living, planning, feeling, willing, righteous, loving Person!

Nor is this cause-and-effect reasoning undermined by the negative things that also exist (e.g., death, hatred, wickedness). These do require a cause to explain them—that is, some basic source of evil in the world. Nevertheless, there is a universal awareness that good is a higher order of reality than evil, and life is better than death.

This awareness must also have a cause. The Creator has allowed evil in the world for a time, so that an even greater good may come in eternity, when all evil is purged and God becomes known as Redeemer, Savior, and Reconciler, as well as Creator.

Primitive Monotheism

This kind of Creator is intuitively recognized in the innermost soul of every human being. A creative, purposeful, caring God would not leave himself without at least some faint witness in the heart of each of his creatures. That witness may have become almost unrecognizable in some cases, having been largely replaced with the practical atheism or the evolutionary pantheism of one's particular culture, but it is—or was—there!

This is true not only in Christian or other monotheistic cultures but also in societies centered around pantheistic or even animistic religions. The ideas of nineteenth century evolutionists such as Comte, Spencer, Tylor, and Frazer have largely been abandoned by modern cultural anthropologists and ethnologists. Those early Darwinians believed that human religions had evolved from animism to ancestor worship to polytheism and, finally, to monotheism. However, the most ancient written records and oral traditions, as well as archaeological excavations, have yielded evidence that all these religions have commonly "devolved" from primitive monotheism to polytheistic pantheism and animism.

Early in their histories, Sumeria, Egypt, and other ancient civilizations became extremely polytheistic and pantheistic; but in each case there is evidence that they originally recognized only one high God. This evidence has been compiled in detail by such scholars as Andrew Lang and Wilhelm Schmidt and is available in summary form in the writings of Samuel Zwemer, Arthur Custance, and others.[1]

The same is true among those tribes and peoples still practicing animistic religions. Although the household gods to which they pray and the spirits which they fear are numerous, they still retain a dim awareness of a great God who created all things. This truth has been documented by missionary scholar Don Richardson[2], and has been corroborated countless times by missionaries working among such tribes—whether in Africa, South America, Oceania, or among the Indians of North America. Furthermore, practically all these peoples retain traditions of the great flood, and many still have distorted recollections of such primeval events as the fall and the dispersion. These records have been preserved for over a hundred generations in oral traditions handed down from one generation to the next.

The tragedy is that although their ancestors knew this true God, their records of him became increasingly distorted with the passing centuries and the pure worship of the Creator eventually became confused with the worship of his creation. All too soon, they began to invest the sun and stars, their ancestors, and finally even the animals with attributes of deity. The host of spirits indwelling and energizing these various created entities were soon being propitiated with prayers and sacrifices, and nature worship became full-fledged idolatry, with images constructed to represent the various gods and goddesses who had evolved out of this progression. The eternal Creator, though still dimly retained in their tribal memories, had been effectively displaced by his creation, and nature had become the source of all things, with its various systems and forces personified by different gods and goddesses. These in turn manifested themselves as spirits that could actually interact with human beings; hence the widespread development of the occult sciences of gurus, witch doctors, and spirit mediums.

All of these pantheistic/polytheistic/animistic religions are evolutionary systems, since they replace the

Creator of the universe with a creating universe, just as do modern scientific evolutionists. Nevertheless, they have not completely displaced the instinctive awareness of the reality of the real Creator God still hidden in the hearts of men and women everywhere.

The Self-Revealing God

Thus far we have noted the strong evidence for the existence of God and a primeval creation of the universe based strictly on science and the secular records of human experience. However, while this approach shows the strong probability of the fact of God, and even something about his necessary attributes, it tells us nothing about his purpose in creation or how we can come to know him in a personal way.

It is reasonable, therefore, to assume that God would reveal his purposes by some means of clear communication to his creatures. Surely the God who created this marvelously complex universe with its thinking, feeling, volitional human beings would not do so capriciously, leaving them to flounder forever, ignorant and unfulfilled. Surely a God like this would reveal himself and his will to those who sincerely desire to know him, no matter where or when they enter the human family.

Such revelation has been accomplished both by inspiration and incarnation, by conveying his Word in written form, and by becoming man himself. Our great God of creation did both, thus giving us two sources of knowledge. His Word has been written down in human language, and he himself became incarnate in human flesh.

There are, of course, many supposedly sacred books in existence, but the Bible is uniquely God's written Word. Other religious writing (e.g., in Buddhism, Confucianism) are based on some form of evolutionary pantheism or even atheism and could certainly not be the revealed Word of the true God of creation whom they deny.

In fact, of all the so-called scriptures of the world's religions, there is only one book which even attempts to expound creation. All others start with the space/time/matter universe already in existence in some primeval form; only the Bible tells how it was called into existence out of nothing except the power of God. It is the only book which actually claims to be the revelation of the Creator; the others do not even acknowledge his existence! The Koran, the Book of Mormon, and a few others do recognize the Creator, but these all explicitly refer to the Old Testament and its Genesis record of creation as their basis for believing in him.

The Bible validates this claim in numerous ways. It is not merely a book of morality or religious philosophy, as are the other sacred books; it is a book of history and fulfilled prophecy. Its accurate accounts are the most detailed and best confirmed histories of the primeval world and of the key events of God's dealings with man. Its hundreds of meticulously fulfilled prophecies are a unique testimonial to its divine origin, and its scientific insights are remarkable. In fact, its very structure offers repeated surprises of design to the Bible student. Although its sixty-six books were written by at least forty different authors over a period of at least fifteen centuries, it has one grand theme: the great purpose of God, from creation to consummation. It is fully consistent both in internal content and external contact, with no provable errors anywhere.

If any book in the world can lay legitimate claim to being the inspired revelation of the world's Creator, that book is the Bible!

Many objective evidences support the claims of the Bible to be the inerrantly inspired Word of God. Within the Bible itself, at least 2,700 times the authors explicitly claim to be writing God's word. (For those interested in further study of these evidences, many books are available on the subject.)[3]

The books of the Bible were originally revealed through the Hebrew, Aramaic, and Greek languages and have since been translated into all the world's key languages. But the Creator not only revealed himself to us in human language; he participated in the human experience by becoming man himself. We can not only read his Word; we can observe his deeds and character. He has become one of us so that we might really come to know him and so that his purpose in creating us can be fulfilled.

This aspect of God's revelation is prophesied in the Old Testament and demonstrated in the New. Unfortunately, even some creationist religions falter at this point. Although they accept God's revelation as Creator, as recorded in the Old Testament, they fail to see that God must also become their Redeemer; thus they reject the central doctrine of the New Testament, namely "that God was in Christ, reconciling the world unto himself" (2 Cor. 5:19).

Before demonstrating that Christ was indeed the incarnate Creator, however, it is necessary to survey the history of God's dealings with the various nations of the world. Where did the nations originate, and why do they have different languages and different religions? Furthermore, why did God select the Hebrew and Greek languages through which to convey his Word to man, and why did he choose to become man through the Jewish nation? These questions play a significant role in understanding God's great purposes for his creation.

God and the Nations

Unfortunately, secular archaeologists and anthropologists speak with discordant voices when they try to describe the primeval ages of human history, especially on matters of chronology. They have been burdened for over a century with the false premise of evolution, and the resultant system of ancient chronology and ethnology is

confused and contradictory. Even under these circum-
stances, however, there have been many correlations of
archaeological discovery with the Bible records.

Dr. Nelson Glueck, often considered the dean of Pal-
estinian archaeologists, though not himself a believer in
biblical inerrancy, says: "No archaeological discovery
has ever controverted a Biblical reference." Then he refers
to the Bible's "almost incredibly correct historical
memory."[4]

God is still God of all the nations, even those that have
rejected or forgotten him. Therefore, only his revealed
Word records the exact truth about history and gives
infallible answers to questions of origins.

The seventy original nations, all coming from the three
sons of the patriarch Noah, are listed in Genesis 10, and
the amazing event that produced these nations is de-
scribed in Genesis 11. In the antediluvian world people
spoke a common language and there were evidently no
organized governments. However, rebellion against the
Creator had entered the very first human family, and
eventually spread so widely that God had to wipe the
world clean with the great flood. Noah and his wife and
their three sons and their wives, along with representa-
tives of each kind of land animal, were the only land-
dwelling survivors, safe in the mighty ark which God told
Noah to build.

It is significant that the ancient story of the flood,
accurately reported in Genesis 6–9, is also found in cor-
rupted form in the records or traditions of nearly every
ancient nation and tribe in the world. This remarkable
fact, well known to ethnologists and anthropologists,
clearly points to a common origin of the post-flood nations, but is almost always ignored by such scientists as
they develop their fanciful theories of human and cultural
evolution.

Furthermore, the great event of the confusion of
tongues and dispersion of the tribes from Babel is also

preserved in many traditions. Different nations and peoples arose as a result of tribal segregation enforced by the miraculous confusion of their languages at Babel (Gen. 11).

The rebellion at Babel which led to this confusion of tongues and subsequent dispersion was centered around the stubborn refusal of the population to separate and "replenish the earth," as God had commanded them to do (Gen. 9:1). Under the leadership of Nimrod, they had "worshipped and served the creature more than the Creator" (Rom. 1:25), with that worship centered in a great temple tower dedicated "unto heaven" (Gen. 11:4). This was the beginning of postdiluvian pantheism, which was soon displayed in astrology and polytheistic idolatry where men honored the "host of heaven" rather than the Creator of heaven.

By supernaturally confounding the languages at Babel, God forced the various families to separate from each other. This dispersion soon resulted in their forming the seventy original nations listed in Genesis 10, and eventually scattering over the entire earth. As a result of this enforced inbreeding over several generations, each family/tribe/nation developed its own distinctive physical characteristics and developed its own peculiar culture, based on the particular geographical resources as well as the ingenuity and industry of the people. Some developed into great civilizations such as Sumeria and Egypt; others eventually degenerated and became extinct like the Neanderthals. These early histories of the dispersing peoples are now being recovered to some extent by archaeological research, but most archaeologists have distorted the records of the relatively few generations involved in these developments into a pseudohistorical fantasy of ape-men evolving over a million years from a hunting-and-gathering semi-animal existence into primitive village economies and finally into civilized societies. All of the factual data of archaeology, however, fit the biblical outline of primeval history far better than this artificial scenario of cultural evolution.

Before the great flood, God dealt with mankind as a unit, all descended from Adam and all speaking the same language. This was still true for a century or more after the flood, with all men descended from Noah and his three sons. Though the population soon departed from God, just as they had before the flood, that severe judgment was a unique, never-to-be-repeated cataclysm. The confusion of tongues and dispersion of people was not another physical cataclysm sent by God; instead, it was a means of enforcing his primeval command to fill the earth and exercise dominion over it.

The problem of human sin and rebellion persisted even after Babel. In fact, each of the scattered tribes carried with them the system of pantheistic worship of the creature rather than the Creator, implemented at Babel under Nimrod; now, however, the names of the "host of heaven" (not merely the stars, but the rebellious angels following Satan in his desire to displace the true God) were expressed in their own new languages as their own pantheons of gods and goddesses. Each of the latter were identified with the different forces and processes of nature which they presumably controlled. Although these early tribes were still aware of the true God, this knowledge gradually became of less and less importance to them in comparison with their own local religious concerns. A classic passage in Paul's prologue to the Book of Romans describes this process so cogently that it needs to be quoted here in its entirety.

> When they knew God, they glorified *him* not as God, neither were thankful; but became vain in their imaginations, and their foolish heart was darkened. Professing themselves to be wise, they became fools, and changed the glory of the uncorruptible God into an image made like to corruptible man, and to birds, and fourfooted beasts, and

creeping things. Wherefore God also gave them up to uncleanness through the lusts of their own hearts, to dishonour their own bodies between themselves: who changed the truth of God into a lie, and worshipped and served the creature more than the Creator, who is blessed for ever. Amen (Rom. 1:21–25).

For two or more centuries after the dispersion, God allowed this widespread delusion to spread, but the true records of his dealings with mankind were still being preserved through Noah's son Shem and his descendants. Finally one of these descendants, Abraham, was chosen to head a new nation, later to be known as Israel and named after Abraham's grandson. Through this nation God once again revealed himself and his purposes for the world; and through this nation he eventually entered the human family.

All of this was essential if God's purpose in creation was to be accomplished. The existing nations had gone off into the beliefs and practices of evolutionary pantheism and were unfit to receive God's revelation, so God prepared a new nation, founded by a man of such strong faith in the true God of creation that he would forever be called "the father of all them that believe" (Rom. 4:11).

Consequently, most of God's written Word would be transmitted to mankind through the medium of the Hebrew language, the tongue of Abraham (Gen. 14:13). The name "Hebrew" probably stemmed from Abraham's ancestor Eber, a great-grandson of Shem; thus, it is at least possible that this was the original language of Noah and Shem, since they had not participated in the Babel rebellion which led to the confusion of tongues. In any case, Hebrew became the language of the Old Testament.

God thenceforth dealt in a particular way with this special nation Israel. He established high moral standards for these people, centered around the Ten Commandments. The children of Israel received great blessings when they obeyed God's Word and great punishments when they disobeyed.

At the same time, God continued—and still continues—to be concerned with all the peoples of the world. The fact is, however, that "both Jews and Gentiles... are all under sin" (Rom. 3:9), for the simple reason that "all have sinned, and come short of the glory of God" (Rom. 3:23).

God's standard can be nothing less than moral perfection, for he is utterly holy and righteous. Yet no one can possibly measure up to that standard. We have all inherited the sinful nature of our first parents, Adam and Eve, and we are all under God's curse of pain and death. "The scripture hath concluded all under sin," and "sin, when it is finished, bringeth forth death" (Gal. 3:22; James 1:15). Both Scripture and science, together with the experience of people in every nation, unite in the sad testimony that "the whole creation groaneth and travaileth in pain together until now" (Rom. 8:22).

The Great Enigma

The patriarch Job, who lived before the establishment of Israel, was surely one of the most righteous men of all time—God himself so testified (Job 1:8; 2:3)—yet Job knew he fell far short. He said: "If I justify myself, mine own mouth shall condemn me: *if I say, I am* perfect, it shall also prove me perverse" (Job 9:20); and so he raised the question: "...but how should man be just with God?" (Job 9:1).

This is the great enigma. God created mankind for himself, in his image, and he has planned a glorious eternal future for them. And since God is the omnipotent, omniscient Creator, he will accomplish this purpose. Yet all men and women are now lost sinners, separated from their Creator because of their own rebellion against him and their inability to satisfy his perfect standards.

None of the various religions among the nations can bridge this gulf, for all of them were developed originally either to counterfeit or to oppose genuine faith in the Creator. The ancient pagan religions, the modern ethnic religions, as well as the many animistic faiths of past and present have no place in their systems for the transcendent, personal, omnipotent God who created the very space/time/matter universe itself. Yet he is the only God who is real!

A number of modern religions, offering a somewhat more sophisticated evolutionism than these older versions of pantheism, include such philosophies as humanism, socialism, existentialism, and the like, but these deny not only the Creator but also all spiritual values; they focus on this world only. Then there are the New Age religions which offer various combinations of pagan mysticism and modern scientism, but which also deny the God of the Bible.

There are even a few religious systems which accept the true God of creation (e.g., Judaism, Islam) but which also fail to bridge the impassable gulf between the all-righteous God and sinful man, for they believe that we can somehow earn his forgiveness and salvation. The fact is, however, that no number of good deeds or holy ceremonies can ever produce perfect righteousness and holiness, and nothing less than this can stand in God's presence. Even Job, that most righteous man of all men, when he finally saw God, could only cry in shame: "I abhor *myself*, and repent in dust and ashes" (Job 42:6).

Sinful men and women can never find salvation through their own efforts or through the religions and philosophies which other sinful men and women have devised. His holiness and justice require that all sin be punished by complete separation from God, but it is obvious that no man could be so punished and also be saved. Yet there can be no salvation unless the sin which keeps us from God is somehow purged and forgiven.

God's purpose cannot be defeated however! Since we are hopelessly separated from him by sin, only God himself can save us! Our Creator must somehow become our Savior.

This great enigma finds its solution in the incarnation: the Creator entering his own world and even human life by becoming a man himself. He became the unique Son of man—perfect man—man as God had intended man to be. Yet, having come from his divine glory, he was also the only begotten Son of God.

As man, he must be born in the prepared nation, Israel, but he could not be born with a sin nature, as all others have been since Adam; and so his human body, like that of Adam, had to be specially "prepared" by God (Heb. 10:5), then "made of a woman" (Gal. 4:4) and born of the virgin, the fulfillment of the ancient promise of the coming seed of the woman who would someday crush Satan and all his works (Gen. 3:15).

This, of course, is the theme of the New Testament, written not in Hebrew, but in Greek, the common language of the world's key nations when the time finally came. The message was to be carried to all nations "that God was in Christ, reconciling the world unto Himself, not imputing their trespasses unto them: and hath committed unto us the word of reconciliation" (2 Cor. 5:18).

5

The God of All Grace

We have shown in earlier chapters that the gods of evolutionism are false gods, whether in the guise of pantheism or of atheism. Special creation by the omnipotent God of the Bible is the only true explanation of the universe. We have also shown that mankind is in rebellion against God, rejecting his Word and seeking to worship and serve the creation instead of the Creator. Therefore, man and his entire dominion are cut off from the only source of real life and ultimate happiness. They are in a state of increasing entropy in which everything is either dead or dying, surviving only on the great, but not inexhaustible, reservoir of life and energy established in the initial creation.

The only remedy for such a sick and dying world was for its Creator himself to intervene. In addition to providing the Bible, his Word, to enable man to understand his situation, God also entered directly into the human family, not only to communicate and interact with mankind, but also to redeem the world from its bondage of sin and death.

The Mystery of Death

No one really understands the phenomenon of death. No one understands why entropy must always increase, even in physical systems, but scientific observation shows that it does. Why people should die at seventy years of age instead of seven hundred, or why they should die at all, is still as mysterious in our scientific age as it was to the pagans of antiquity. Gerontologists may study the aging process and discourse learnedly about biological clocks and somatic mutations, but they cannot stop the process. Medical researchers may eliminate many of the diseases that lead to death, but they cannot cure the greater disease of death itself.

Mankind's greatest fear is the fear of death; his greatest grief is grief over the death of a loved one. Death is the great enemy, and the plaintive cry of the ancient patriarch echoes through the centuries down the valley of the shadow of death: "If a man die, shall he live *again?*" (Job 14:14).

The answers of the pantheistic and animistic religions are as vague as their evolutionary concepts of origins. They may speak of the spirit departing from a dead body into some strange world of spirits, or transmigrating into the body of some future being, or being swallowed up in the all-soul of the cosmos, or evolving into some higher sphere of spiritual awareness, or some other vague concept of immortality. In none of these religions of evolutionary pantheism, however, is there any promise of a resurrection of the body and a continuation of the whole person—spirit, soul, and body—into endless life. They have all rejected the Creator of life and can therefore offer no hope of a real resurrection of physical life—only a shadowy "after-life," or nothing at all.

Only the creationist religions (Judaism, Islam, Christianity) speak of a resurrection, because only the Creator of life can conquer death and because death is above all his own condemnation of man's rebellion against him. However, both Judaism and Islam fail to discern the all-important necessity for God to become one of us and then die in our place if we are ever to be delivered from the bondage of sin and death.

The Old Testament had so little to say about the resurrection, in fact, that one prominent sect of the Jews, the Sadducees, denied it altogether. Nevertheless, it was there. (Note Daniel 12:2, for example: "Many of them that sleep in the dust of the earth shall awake, some to everlasting life, and some to shame *and* everlasting contempt.")

Mohammed's Koran, on the other hand, as well as the commentaries of later Moslem theologians, make the future resurrection and its fiery judgment almost as prominent a doctrine as their foundational doctrine of Allah's creation of the world. They even accept many distinctively Christian doctrines, most notably the virgin birth of Jesus and his future return to Earth. Nevertheless, the Moslems, like the Jews, reject the all-important doctrines of his deity, atoning death, and bodily resurrection. Although the Koran has much to say about a future resurrection, it appears there only as a part of the supposed revelations received by one man, Mohammed, who himself died soon thereafter and is still in the grave, conquered by death like all other men and women since Adam.

There is one exception to this statement, one supremely important exception! The Jews and Muslims and all the evolutionary religionists may deny it, but the fact is that Jesus Christ has already conquered the great enemy death. He was a man as well as the Creator, and he did die as a man; but he rose again bodily from the grave, thus validating all his claims and guaranteeing all his wonderful promises of salvation.

Since only the God of creation can create life, only he can defeat death.

The Resurrection of Christ

Death may be a great enigma, as well as the great enemy, but it is no mystery to one who believes the Bible. "The wages of sin is death," the Bible says (Rom. 6:23). Because the father of all people, Adam, sinned, rebelling against God, and thus denying his sovereignty as Creator, God had to separate himself from Adam and all his children. "Wherefore, as by one man sin entered into the world, and death by sin; and so death passed upon all men, for that all have sinned" (Rom. 5:12).

Thus, deliverance from death required deliverance from sin. This could only be accomplished by a man who was himself without sin offering himself as a substitutionary sacrifice, one who could pay the wages of sin on behalf of all those who were sinners, letting them go free. None but God himself could meet these conditions.

One could ask a legitimate question here: "Assuming this to be true, how do we know who is really God? There have been many religions, and many great religious leaders. How can we decide which one is truly God's representative, or God himself?"

The answer is found in another question: "Knowing that only God could conquer death, what great teacher, sinless man, worker of miracles and religious leader died, was buried, then later rose alive from the grave, never to die again, thus demonstrating that he was indeed God manifest in the flesh?" Only one person in all of history has ever claimed to meet this seemingly impossible criterion.

> God anointed Jesus of Nazareth with the Holy Ghost and with power: who went about doing good, and healing all that were oppressed of the devil; for God was with him. And we are witnesses of all things which he did both in the land of the Jews, and in Jerusalem; whom they slew and hanged on a tree: him God raised up the third day, and

shewed him openly; Not to all the people, but unto wit-
nesses chosen before of God, *even* to us, who did eat and
drink with him after he rose from the dead (Acts 10:38–41).

The resurrection of Jesus Christ is the most important
event since creation itself. It demonstrates that Jesus of
Nazareth was actually God in human flesh, the God-man.
As the only sinless man, his death was a substitutionary
act, offered in sacrifice for the sins of the whole world and
satisfying both the requirements of divine justice and the
fullness of God's loving purpose.

Naturally, such a tremendous event, assuring the fulfillment of all God's purposes in creation, would be opposed by Satan and all those whose own purposes would
be destroyed thereby. Consequently, the truth of Christ's
resurrection has been denied by evolutionists of all varieties, not only the atheists and humanists of the modern
scientific/educational establishments, but also by the religious leaders of every religion in the world except biblical
Christianity. Even the creationist religions of Judaism
and Islam reject it, as well as liberal and cultic "Christian" theologians and teachers who themselves have sur-
rendered to evolutionism.

Nevertheless, the evidence supporting the truth of
Christ's resurrection is as strong or stronger than any
other fact in history. Multitudes of Christian men and
women, from the times of Christ to this modern day, have
trusted their lives and souls to him as their Creator and
Savior, receiving assurance of sins forgiven and everlasting life through faith in his Word. With the apostle
Peter they would all testify that they have been "begotten. . . again unto a lively hope by the resurrection of
Jesus Christ from the dead" (1 Peter 1:3) and, like Peter,
they would insist that "we have not followed cunningly
devised fables" (2 Peter 1:16).

To the claim, as made by some, that the whole story of
Jesus and his resurrection was some kind of "passover

plot," concocted by his disciples for their own selfish purposes, they would point out that all his disciples, plus multitudes of their followers, were so persuaded of the reality of his resurrection that they continued to preach it courageously, even when it cost them their own lives. Men and women would never suffer and die willingly for some tale they knew (or even suspected) to be false.

There can be no question that Jesus' disciples and other early Christians believed with utmost sincerity, sealed in blood, that he had risen from the dead. They who had the unique opportunity to examine all the evidences and all the testimonies firsthand, and who had every possible incentive to reject them if they were invalid, believed them and preached the resurrection as long as they lived. And they changed the world!

Many non-Christians have been willing to acknowledge the sincerity of these first Christians, but argue that they were wrong nonetheless. These skeptics imagine that the disciples were gullible and so anxious to believe Jesus was still with them after his death that they suffered hallucinations and saw visions which they finally came to believe.

Such notions are themselves a testimony to the gullibility, not of the disciples, but of the skeptics. Listen to the apostle Paul, one of the most brilliant logicians and best-trained minds of the world of that day.

> For I delivered unto you first of all that which I also received, how that Christ died for our sins according to the scriptures; and that he was buried, and that he rose again the third day according to the scriptures: and that he was seen of Cephas, then of the twelve: after that, he was seen of above five hundred brethren at once; of whom the greater part remain unto this present, but some are fallen asleep. After that, he was seen of James; then of all the apostles (1 Cor. 15:3–7).

There are at least ten different occasions recorded in Scripture when Christ appeared to one or more of his disciples after his resurrection. Sometimes it was indoors; sometimes it was outdoors. Sometimes he appeared to one or two; several times he appeared to all the disciples; at least once he appeared to a large crowd. He ate with them and talked with them; his body still had the nailprints and the wound of the spear inflicted during the crucifixion. No visions or hallucinations were ever like this!

Some critics have imagined that he only swooned on the cross, then recovered in the tomb, removed the great weight of grave clothes and spices tightly wound around his body, rolled away the great stone, overpowered the guards at the tomb, and then returned triumphantly to his fearful disciples. Such a fanciful story is its own refutation.

Some have said Mary Magdalene went to the wrong tomb, despite the fact that it was a freshly constructed tomb with no others nearby. Some have thought the disciples stole the body while others say the Jews or the Romans moved the body. All such attempts to explain away the empty tomb founder on the fact that the body could not be produced later. Both Jews and Romans did everything they could to stamp out the spreading flame of Christianity, and the best way to do it would have been merely to display the corpse of Jesus to the multitudes who were believing and preaching his resurrection. This they could never do, however, for that body had ascended alive into heaven forty days after his resurrection.

Jesus had, indeed, "shewed himself alive after his passion by many infallible proofs, being seen of them forty days, and speaking of the things pertaining to the kingdom of God" (Acts 1:3). No one has ever been able to refute these proofs, though many have tried. Many large volumes have been published over the years in defense of the great truth that the Lord Jesus Christ died and rose again; and they have never been refuted.

One should consider the significance of this truth: the most important fact of history is the best-proved fact of history, despite all that the enemies of God could do to prevent or deny it. Confucius is dead. Buddha is dead. Lao-tze is dead. Mohammed is dead. Darwin is dead. Marx is dead.

But Jesus is alive! In his present, resurrected, glorified physical body, he appeared to the beloved disciple John and said: " . . . Fear not; I am the first and the last: *I am* he that liveth, and was dead; and, behold, I am alive for evermore, Amen; and have the keys of hell and of death" (Rev. 1:17–18).

By his resurrection, he has demonstrated himself to be the Son of God, the creator and ruler of all things. When the apostle Paul preached to the intellectuals in Athens, the greatest cultural and religious center of the world where evolutionary philosophers (e.g., Stoics, Platonists, Epicureans, Gnostics) held sway and polytheists and pantheists abounded as never before or since, he challenged them with the following words.

God that made the world and all things therein, seeing that he is Lord of heaven and earth, dwelleth not in temples made with hands; neither is worshipped with men's hands, as though he needed any thing, seeing he giveth to all life, and breath, and all things; and hath made of one blood all nations of men for to dwell on all the face of the earth, and hath determined the times before appointed, and the bounds of their habitation; that they should seek the Lord, if haply they might feel after him, and find him, though he be not far from every one of us: for in him we live, and move, and have our being; as certain also of your own poets have said, For we are also his offspring. Forasmuch then as we are the offspring of God, we ought not to think that the Godhead is like unto gold, or silver, or stone, graven by art and man's device. And the times of this ignorance God winked at; but now commandeth all men everywhere to repent: because he hath appointed a day, in which he will judge the world in righteousness by *that* man whom he hath ordained; *whereof* he hath given assurance unto all *men* in that he hath raised him from the dead (Acts 17:24–31).

This great sermon to the Athenians tells it all. God, the creator of all things and the ruler of all the nations, has manifested himself as an ordained Man who will judge the world. He has validated his claims by conquering the great enemy with his resurrection from the dead, making possible the reconciliation of all nations to their maker. For a time God has "winked" at the religions that have replaced the Creator with his creation, but that time is past, and all must now return to the true God or be judged in righteousness by the God-man who has defeated sin and death and now offers forgiveness and eternal life.

The Grace of God

"For the grace of God that bringeth salvation hath appeared to all men" (Titus 2:11). When God became man and the Creator became the Savior, he called himself "the Son of man" (Matt. 8:20). Although he entered humanity through the Jewish nation and his first followers were almost all Jews, he came with great love and concern for all nations.

In the beginning was the Word, and the Word was with God, and the Word was God.... All things were made by him: and without him was not any thing made that was made. In him was life; and the life was the light of men.... *That* was the true Light, which lighteth every man that cometh into the world. He was in the world, and the world was made by him, and the world knew him not" (John 1:1, 3–4, 9–10).

He is not only the God of all creation; he is the God of all grace. He created men and women in his own image, with the glorious purpose that "in the ages to come he might shew the exceeding riches of his grace in *his* kindness toward us through Christ Jesus" (Eph. 2:7).

This purpose had been seemingly thwarted by human sin and rebellion, which resulted in the agelong dominance of evolutionary humanism in all its variations, accompanied in varying degrees by every imaginable form of moral wickedness that could be devised by men and women separated from God.

> And even as they did not like to retain God in *their* knowledge, God gave them over to a reprobate mind, . . . being filled with all unrighteousness, fornication, wickedness, covetousness, maliciousness; full of envy, murder, debate, deceit, malignity; whisperers, backbiters, haters of God, despiteful, proud, boasters, inventors of evil things, disobedient to parents, without understanding, covenant-breakers, without natural affection, implacable, unmerciful: who knowing the judgment of God, that they which commit such things are worthy of death, not only do the same, but have pleasure in them that do them (Rom. 1:28–32).

This terrible description and awful indictment by the apostle Paul describes the pagan world of antiquity, but it fits equally well in our modern age. "As it is written, there is none righteous, no, not one: there is none that understandeth, there is none that seeketh after God. They are all gone out of the way, they are together become unprofitable; there is none that doeth good, no, not one" (Rom. 3:10–12).

This universal indictment is written, of course, from the perspective of a God of perfect purity and holiness before whom the whole world stands condemned, deserving nothing but eternal banishment from God's presence and endless punishment for rejecting his love. This is what we all merit, both because of the sinful natures with which we were born and the rebellious deeds, words, and thoughts which we manifest daily in our lives.

The holy God of creation must punish sin and banish sin, and all of us are lost sinners before him. Yet he is also the loving God of grace and the God of unfailing purpose. The only solution for the great dilemma is Jesus Christ, the incarnate Word, who is himself the measure of God's infinite grace and mercy.

> For ye know the grace of our Lord Jesus Christ, that, though he was rich, yet for your sakes he became poor, that ye through his poverty might be rich (2 Cor. 8:9).
>
> For Christ also hath once suffered for sins, the just for the unjust, that He might bring us to God (1 Peter 3:18).
>
> For God so loved the world, that he gave his only begotten Son, that whosoever believeth in him should not perish, but have everlasting life (John 3:16).

No wonder the Scriptures call our Creator "the God of all grace, who hath called us unto his eternal glory by Christ Jesus" (1 Peter 5:10). He who was rich became poor for us. He who knew no sin was made sin for us (2 Cor. 5:21). He who is life itself died for us! "For all have sinned, and come short of the glory of God; being justified freely by his grace through the redemption that is in Christ Jesus" (Rom. 3:23, 24).

The Christian faith is, thus, not merely one religion among many. It is the true revelation of the one true God of creation, the record of his provision of forgiveness and salvation. All human religions betray their humanistic origin by their humanly attainable standards, whereas God's way of salvation is by his grace, received only by faith. "Not by works of righteousness which we have done, but according to his mercy he saved us...that being justified by his grace, we should be made heirs according to the hope of eternal life" (Titus 3:5, 7).

The Bible, the true Word of God, gives the only account of the creation of the universe, then reports the only resurrection from the dead, and finally uniquely reveals God's grace in providing salvation by faith apart from works, recognizing the impossibility of attaining God's perfect standard by human effort. The Lord Jesus Christ, our Creator and Redeemer, gives eternal life to all who trust their souls to him.

Alive in Christ

A true Christian is a person who is "in Christ," one who has identified himself with Jesus Christ in his death and resurrection, acknowledging that Christ died for his sins and rose again for his justification before a holy God. Thus he becomes dead to his old life of rebellion against his Creator and alive to a new life of fellowship and walking daily with his Lord. As Paul said: "I am crucified with Christ: nevertheless I live: yet not I, but Christ liveth in me: and the life which I now live in the flesh I live by the faith of the Son of God, who loved me, and gave himself for me" (Gal. 2:20).

The Christian life becomes, therefore, the life of Christ himself indwelling and energizing believers through the Spirit of God who unites them in an eternal bond the very moment they trust Christ for forgiveness and salvation. The life of Christ, of course, having once died for sin, and been raised again, is now eternal resurrection life. Christ promises: ". . . He that heareth my word, and believeth on him that sent me, hath everlasting life, and shall not come into condemnation; but is passed from death unto life" (John 5:24). Christ's everlasting life becomes a present possession of true believers, transforming the quality of their lives in this present age, carrying them through death into the personal presence of Christ in heaven, reuniting them with their resurrected bodies when Christ returns to earth, and ultimately taking them on into the endless ages of a perfected cosmos when God's purposes in creation have all been accomplished.

This is not merely religion; it is real living! The God of the Bible, revealed in Christ, is the real God, and he who created us is also the one who redeems us. This is the real purpose for which God created men and women in his own "image" (Gen. 1:27), that he might walk daily in fellowship with them, eternally bestowing his grace and love on them, receiving their love and fruitful service in happy response.

The Christian life indeed is one of "joy and peace in believing" (Rom. 15:13). At the same time, it is also a life of service and witness, conflict and persecution, suffering and death (Luke 9:23). Though believers have been reconciled to God, they must still live for the present in a world that is in bitter rebellion against its Creator. Even when God "was in the world, and the world was made by him . . . the world knew him not" (John 1:10), and they "crucified the Lord of glory" (1 Cor. 2:8). Jesus said, therefore, " . . . because ye are not of the world, but I have chosen you out of the world, therefore the world hateth you" (John 15:19). Nevertheless, we must follow Christ, for he said: "He that taketh not his cross, and followeth after me, is not worthy of me. He that findeth his life shall lose it: and he that loseth his life for my sake shall find it" (Matt. 10:38, 39).

Not only do Christians have the world and the devil to oppose them, however; they must also contend with their own fleshly natures. Though the new nature has been implanted by the Holy Spirit, the old nature is still present as well, and there will necessarily be a mortal conflict between the two. We must continually strive to "put off . . . the old man . . . and . . . put on the new man, which after God is created in righteousness and true holiness" (Eph. 4:22, 24), " . . . the new *man*, which is renewed in knowledge after the image of him that created him" (Col. 3:10).

We are not without adequate resources in the conflict, of course. We have the indwelling presence of God himself in the person of his Holy Spirit, and we can daily look to him for strength and guidance. We have the holy Scriptures, and we should study them daily. The concluding exhortation of the apostle Paul climaxed in these mighty words: "All scripture *is* given by inspiration of God, and *is* profitable for doctrine, for reproof, for correction, for instruction in righteousness: that the man of God may be perfect, throughly furnished unto all good works" (2 Tim. 3:16–17).

There is also the tremendous resource of prayer. The Lord Jesus promised: "Whatsoever ye shall ask in my name, that will I do, that the Father may be glorified in the Son" (John 14:13). And Paul said: ". . . in every thing by prayer and supplication with thanksgiving let your requests be made known unto God. And the peace of God, which passeth all understanding, shall keep your hearts and minds through Christ Jesus" (Phil. 4:6–7).

Finally, the encouragement and fellowship of other Christians is vitally important, along with the teaching and exhortation of Christian leaders. These are available mainly through the church, especially the congregation of like-minded believers in one's own local community. Each new Christian, therefore, should immediately unite with a Bible-believing, Bible-teaching local church, openly confessing Christ as Savior and Lord by baptism and by regular participation in the fellowship and ministries of the church. All of these resources will strengthen believers in the faith, equipping them for the conflict, enabling them to live godly Christian lives, blessing their families, giving them a fruitful ministry and, in general, preparing them for a still greater life of service for their Creator/Savior in the ages to come.

The God of Eternity

This present age will be over soon and, as Paul has said: ". . . the sufferings of this present time *are* not worthy *to be compared* with the glory that shall be revealed in us" (Rom. 8:18). The future age is not one of some vague immortality of souls, as the world's evolutionist religions envision, but one of heavenly glory. God's purpose in creation must eventually be accomplished, for he cannot fail. His creation of our magnificent cosmos was not capricious and tentative, but purposeful and eternal.

"They that be wise shall shine as the brightness of the firmament; and they that turn many to righteousness as the stars for ever and ever" (Dan. 12:3). "I know that, whatsoever God doeth, it shall be for ever: nothing can be put to it, nor any thing taken from it: and God doeth *it*, that *men* should fear before him" (Eccl. 3:14).

As the first book of the Bible records the events of the first ages, so the last book records those of the final ages. Further, as the first two chapters of Genesis describe the creation, so the last two chapters of Revelation describe the glorious consummation. The creation assures the consummation and, because rebellious men fear the consummation, they labor hard to deny the creation. This is why, of all the sixty-six books of the Bible, Genesis and Revelation have always been under the greatest attack by humanistic philosophers, pseudoscientists, false prophets, and corrupt teachers. Nevertheless, these two "bookends" of the Bible are infallible histories of things past and things to come, revealed by God for our instruction and guidance concerning our own part in his eternal plan.

(The reader may wish to refer to my verse-by-verse commentaries on these two key books: *The Genesis Record* (Baker, 1976) and *The Revelation Record* (Tyndale, 1983). These are devotional in tone, literal in exposition, narrative and simple in style, and scientific in accuracy.)

As we have shown in earlier chapters, the various religions and philosophies of the world are not really the
various paths by which men and women are seeking God.
Rather they are the products of the humanistic reasonings
by which men have sought to escape, or even to oblit-
erate, the true God of creation. Most religions deny that
such a Creator even exists and the others purport to pull
him down to a level which human beings can reach by
their own efforts. Such evolutionary and man-deifying
systems have unleashed a Pandora's box of conflict, suffering, and wickedness on mankind.

Nevertheless, all real facts of science, history, and human experience support the unique biblical revelation of
special creation by a transcendent yet immanent, omnipotent, omniscient, holy yet loving, personal Creator
God. Furthermore, the variegated religions of the world
still retain a dim awareness of such a God at the dawn of
their history, regardless of how far they have departed
from him now. Deep within the soul of each person,
whatever his or her tribal or national religion, there is
still the consciousness that somewhere there is a God
who cares and who is real.

That real God, the God of creation, became a real man
in the person of Jesus Christ and paid the awful price of
the world's redemption by his substitutionary death for
the sin of the world. The sufficiency of his death and the
truth of his deity have been demonstrated by his unique
victory over death, sin, and Satan when he rose bodily
from the grave, never to die again. The great enemy has
been defeated, and Christ can now assure forgiveness and
eternal salvation of body, soul, and spirit to all who receive him by personal faith as Creator, Savior, Lord and
coming King.

For he is coming to Earth again! He is at the throne of
God in heaven now, in his resurrection body, though he is
also present with his people here on Earth in the person of
the Holy Spirit. One day—perhaps very soon—"the Lord

himself shall descend from heaven. . . and the dead in Christ shall rise first: then we which are alive *and* remain shall be caught up together with them in the clouds, to meet the Lord in the air: and so shall we ever be with the Lord" (1 Thess. 4:16, 17).

This is not the place to discuss details of the prophetic Scriptures. Sincere Bible-believing Christians still differ with one another on certain aspects of prophetic interpretation, as they do on various other teachings of the Bible, and so they have formed different denominations and schools of interpretation. Nevertheless, the Bible is clear, and most Bible-believing Christians agree, on the basic doctrines related to creation, redemption, and consummation as summarized in this book. God will, indeed, fulfill his purposes in creation and redemption when Christ comes again.

This will include a bodily resurrection of believers and a transformation of the bodies of those still living at that time. Our bodies will be "fashioned like unto his glorious body" (Phil. 3:21), and there will be "no more death, neither sorrow, nor crying, neither shall there be any more pain: for the former things are passed away" (Rev. 21:4).

The Earth itself shall eventually be purged of its bondage to decay when the very "elements shall melt with fervent heat"; God will then call forth from these purified elements "a new earth, wherein dwelleth righteousness" (2 Peter 3:10, 13). The law of entropy will be repealed, and the whole creation will finally "be delivered from the bondage of corruption into the glorious liberty of the children of God" (Rom. 8:21). "And there shall be no more curse. . . his servants shall serve him" (Rev. 22:3).

With sin removed from both our transformed bodies and the purified world forever, we shall, indeed, be free to "serve him" in the "new heaven" and "new earth" (Rev. 21:1) for all the ages to come. With the unbounded space, endless time, and innumerable worlds of God's creation at hand, our eternal service under the direction of our great Creator and loving Savior will be challenging, fascinating, and fruitful forever!

On the other hand, the multitudes who die in their sins, rejecting his wonderful gospel of salvation and redeeming grace, will be lost forever, "punished with everlasting destruction from the presence of the Lord, and from the glory of his power" (2 Thess. 1:9). It is my fervent prayer that no readers of these lines will ever end up in this company, separated forever from the fulfillment of God's purpose in their creation.

Instead, I pray that many readers will open their hearts and minds to the God who is real, the God who created them, the God who, in Christ, died to save them and rose again from the dead to assure them eternal life.

The grace of God is freely bestowed—that's what grace is—on all who believe. You that are longing to see his face, will you this moment his grace receive?

Notes

Chapter 1. The Impotent God of Chance

1. Julian Huxley, in *Issues in Evolution*, ed. Sol Tax (Chicago: University of Chicago Press, 1960), 45.

2. Julian Huxley, *Evolution in Action* (New York: Harper Brothers, 1953), 42.

3. Francis Crick, *Life Itself* (New York: Simon and Schuster, 1981), 51.

4. Ibid., 88.

5. Hubert P. Yockey, "Self-Organization Origin of Life Scenarios and Information Theory," *Journal of Theoretical Biology* 91 (1981): 27.

6. Hubert P. Yockey, "A Calculation of the Probability of Spontaneous Biogenesis by Information Theory," *Journal of Theoretical Biology* 67 (1977): 398.

7. Richard Dawkins, "What Was All the Fuss About?" *Nature* 316 (22 August 1985): 683.

8. Colin Patterson, "Cladistics." Interview on BBC with Peter Franz, 4 March 1982.

9. Niles Eldredge, *Time Frames* (New York: Simon and Schuster, 1985), 33.

10. Pierre P. Grassè, *Evolution of Living Organisms* (New York: Academic Press, 1977), 103.

11. Ibid., 107.

12. Keith Stewart Thomson, "The Meaning of Evolution," *American Scientist* 70 (September/October 1982): 529.

13. Paul Kurtz, "An Interview with Isaac Asimov on Science and the Bible," *Free Inquiry* 2 (Spring 1982): 8.

Chapter 2. The Immoral Gods of Pantheism

1. Ilza Veith, "Creation and Evolution in the Far East," in *Issues in Evolution*, ed. Sol Tax (Chicago: University of Chicago Press, 1960), 1–2.

2. Michael Ruse, "The Long March of Darwin," review of *China and Charles Darwin*, by J.R. Pusey, *New Scientist* 103 (16 August 1984): 35.

3. Michael Denton, *Evolution: A Theory in Crisis* (London: Burnett Books, Ltd., 1985), 37.

4. Ibid.

5. George Wald, "A Knowing Universe Seeking to be Known," reported by D.E. Thomsen, *Science News* 123 (19 February 1983):124.

6. George Gale, "The Anthropic Principle," *Scientific American* 245 (December 1981): 154.

7. Judith Hooper, "Perfect Timing," *New Age Journal* 11 (December 1985):18.

8. Fritjof Capra, "The Dance of Life," *Science Digest* 90 (April 1982):33.

9. Jeremy Rifkin, *Algeny* (New York: Viking Press, 1983), 188.

10. Francisco Ayala, "Nothing in Biology Makes Sense Except in the Light of Evolution: Theodosius Dobzhansky, 1900–1975," *Journal of Heredity* 68, no. 3 (1977):3.

11. Ibid., 9.

12. Ibid., 6.

13. Rifkin, *Algeny*, 244.

14. Julian Huxley, "A New World Vision," *The Humanist* 39 (March/April 1979):36.

15. Ibid., 37.

16. Ibid., 38.

17. Richard Wurmbrand, *Marx and Satan* (Westchester, Illinois: Crossway Books, 1986), 143.

18. Kenneth J. Hsu, "Darwin's Three Mistakes," *Geology* 14 (June 1986):534.

19. Rifkin, *Algeny*, 255.

Chapter 3. Science and the God of Creation

1. Jeremy Cherfas, "The Difficulties of Darwinism," *New Scientist* 102 (17 May 1984):29. This article is a report by science writer Cherfas of the important Tanner Lecture given by Harvard's Stephen Jay Gould at Cambridge University in 1984.

2. Ibid.

3. Denton, *Theory in Crisis*, 100. This book by an Australian research molecular geneticist is not a creationist book, but is an incisive critique of most aspects of evolutionary theory.

4. Tom Kemp, "A Fresh Look at the Fossil Record," *New Scientist* 108 (5 December 1985):67.

5. Steven M. Stanley, *Macroevolution: Pattern and Process* (San Francisco: W.M. Freeman and Co., 1979), 39.

6. Stephen Jay Gould, "Is a New and General Theory of Evolution Emerging?" *Paleobiology* 6, no. 1 (1980):127. Dr. Gould and Dr. Niles Eldredge, of the American Museum, are leaders in the modern "punctuated equilibrium" school of thought among evolutionists.

7. Denton, *Theory in Crisis*, 160.

8. S.J. Gould and N. P. Eldredge, "Punctuated Equilibria: The Tempo and Mode of Evolution Reconsidered," *Paleobiology* 3 (Spring 1977):147.

9. "The Oldest Fossil Bird: A Rival for *Archaeopteryx*," *Science* 129 (20 January 1978):284; Tim Beardsley, "Fossil Bird Shakes Evolutionary Hypotheses," *Nature* 322 (1986):677; Fred Hoyle and Chandra Wickramasinghe,

Archaeopteryx: The Primordial Bird (Swansea, Wales: Christopher Davies, Ltd, 1986), 135.

10. Denton, *Theory in Crisis*, 180.

11. Tom Kemp, "The Reptiles that Became Mammals," *New Scientist* 93 (4 March 1982):583.

12. Steven Stanley, "Resetting the Evolutionary Timetable," interview by Neil A. Campbell, *Bioscience* 36 (December 1986):726.

13. Rifkin, *Algeny*, 125.

14. Mark Ridley, "Who Doubts Evolution?" *New Scientist* 90 (25 June 1981):831.

15. Richard Morris, *Time's Arrow: Scientific Attitudes Toward Time* (New York: Simon and Schuster, 1984), 212.

16. Gordon J. Van Wylen and Richard E. Sonntag, *Fundamentals of Classical Thermodynamics* (New York: Wiley, 1982), 271. The senior author of this treatise was, at the time of writing, Dean of Engineering at the University of Michigan.

17. George P. Stravropoulos, Letter to the Editor, *American Scientist* 65 (November/December 1977):675.

18. Daniel R. Brooks and E.D. Wiley, *Evolution in Entropy* (Chicago: University of Chicago Press, 1986), 335.

19. Ibid., 43.

20. Ibid., 70.

21. Joseph Felsenstein, "Waiting for Post-New-Darwin Evolution," *Evolution* 40, no. 4 (1986):887.

22. Ibid., 888.

23. Brian Charlesworth, "Entropy: The Great Illusion," *Evolution* 40, no. 4 (1986):879–880.

Chapter 4. The God of the Bible

1. Samuel M. Zwemer, *The Origin of Religion* (New York: Loiseaux Brothers, 1945), 256. Dr. Zwemer was Professor of History of Religion at Princeton and a missionary statesman. Arthur C. Custance, *Evolution or Creation*; Part II, "Primitive Monotheism and the Origin

of Polytheism" (Grand Rapids: Zondervan Publishing House, 1976), 110–139. See also the chapter on "Primitive Cultures" by Dr. Custance in his book *Genesis and Early Man* (Grand Rapids: Zondervan Publishing House, 1975), pp. 60–143.

2. Don Richardson, *Eternity in Their Hearts* (Ventura, California: Regal Books, 1981), 176.

3. Henry M. Morris, *Many Infallible Proofs* (San Diego: Creation-Life Publishers, 1974), 381.

4. Nelson Glueck, *Rivers in the Desert* (New York: Farrar, Straus and Cudahy, 1959), 31.

For Further Reading

If you would like to study further the topics briefly discussed in *The God Who is Real*, the following books by the same author are suggested:

Evidences of Christianity

Many Infallible Proofs (Master Books, 1974, 381 pp.). Readable, yet authoritative, exposition of the many evidences of the inspiration of the Bible, the deity of Christ, and the truth of the Christian gospel. Evidences from history, prophecy, science, and other fields, with answers to the supposed difficulties and objections. Widely used as a textbook.

The Biblical Basis for Modern Science (Baker Book House, 1984, 516 pp.). A complete reference book on the scientific evidences for the inerrancy and authority of the Bible, with chapters on each of the sciences (astronomy, geology, etc.) in its biblical context, plus separate chapters on special topics (miracles, etc.) Many illustrations, appendices, and indexes.

Creation/Evolution

Scientific Creationism (Master Books, Second Edition, 1985, 281 pp.). The book generally regarded as the definitive treatment of the modern scientific case for creation and against evolution. Final chapter deals in depth with the biblical doctrine of creation; all others contain only scientific material.

The Twilight of Evolution (Baker Book House, 1963, 103 pp.). A concise summary of the scientific and moral case against evolutionism. Widely influential in the modern revival of creationism during the past quarter century.

Creation Evangelism

Creation and the Modern Christian (Master Books, 1985, 298 pp.). Shows the foundational importance of the doctrine of special creation in every phase of Christian truth and life, with documented proof of the harmful effects of evolutionism everywhere.

King of Creation (Master Books, 1980, 239 pp.). Biblical and scientific insights into the vital importance of creationism in Christian evangelism, missions, and discipleship. Foreword by Josh McDowell.

The Troubled Waters of Evolution (Master Books, 1975, 217 pp.). The long and troubled history of evolutionism, from ancient paganism to modern neo-Darwinism, with special emphasis on its bitter fruits in the modern world.

Biblical Studies in Ancient History

The Genesis Record (Baker Book House, 1976, 716 pp.). Complete commentary on the Book of Genesis, with devotional, Christ-centered emphasis in easy-to-read narrative exposition. Thorough treatment of all relevant scientific and historical questions and problems.

The Remarkable Record of Job (Baker Book House, 1988, 146 pp.). Scientific and devotional study of the Bible's oldest and most fascinating book, noting the many remarkable scientific, historical, and theological insights not found in other commentaries.

Christian Faith and Life

The Bible Has the Answer (Baker Book House, 1976, 394 pp.). Logical, biblical, scientific answers to one hundred of the most vital and frequently asked questions regarding the Bible and Christian life.

Publishers' Addresses

Master Books, Box 1606, El Cajon, CA 92022; (619) 448-1121

Baker Book House, P.O. Box 6287, Grand Rapids, MI 49516-6287

Scripture Index

Name and Subject Index